The Manhattan Diaries Series

Unlock Manhattan
Master the Art of Lasting Impressions

Manhattan Allure
Just Like That

The Manhattan Diaries Series

Manhattan Allure ~ Just Like That

Manhattan Vitality ~ Just Like That

Manhattan Lifestyle ~ Just Like That

Manhattan Ambition ~ Just Like That

The Manhattan Diaries Series

Unlock Manhattan
Master the Art of Lasting Impressions

Manhattan Allure
Just Like That

NATALIE LOGAN

L

Urban Chronicles Publishing House
an imprint of The Ridge Publishing Group
Coeur d'Alene, Idaho, U.S.A.

DISCLAIMER: The ideas, concepts, and opinions expressed in The Manhattan Diaries Series (hereinafter referred to as "Series") are intended to help readers make thoughtful and informed decisions about their lifestyle. This Series is sold with the understanding that author and publisher are not rendering medical advice of any kind, nor is this Series intended to replace the medical advice, nor to diagnose, prescribe, or treat any disease, condition, illness, or injury. It should not be used as a substitute for treatment by or the advice of a professional healthcare provider. It is recommended that before beginning any diet or exercise program, including any aspect of the Series, you receive full medical clearance from a licensed healthcare provider. Although the author and publisher have endeavored to ensure that the information provided in the Series is complete and accurate, the author and publisher claim no responsibility to any person or entity for any liability, loss, or damage caused or alleged to be caused directly or indirectly as a result of the use, application, or interpretation of the material in this Series, or any errors or omissions in the Series.

CREDIT: This book was written with limited assistance of ChatGPT, an AI language model developed by OpenAI. The collaboration provided unique insights and support in crafting content. The book cover was created using Midjourney tools and Adobe Photoshop, ensuring a visually captivating design.

Library of Congress Control Number: 2024916248

Unlock Manhattan: Master the Art of Lasting Impressions by Natalie Logan

ISBN: 978-1-956905-09-0 (e-book)
ISBN: 978-1-956905-10-6 (Softcover)

1. Social Science / Popular Culture. 2. Self-Help / Personal Growth / Success. 3. Self-Help / Motivational & Inspirational. 4. Fashion & Beauty / Fashion. I. Title. II. Series.

First Edition: August 2024

Printed in the United States of America

Contents

The Manhattan Diaries Series

DARE TO REIMAGINE YOURSELF . . .

21 Steps to Reinvent and Discover a Side of You Manhattan's Never Seen

The Manhattan Diaries Series presents:

Manhattan Allure—Just Like That mini-series (books 1–5)

Manhattan Vitality—Just Like That mini-series (books 6–10)

Manhattan Lifestyle—Just Like That mini-series (books 11–16)

Manhattan Ambition—Just Like That mini-series (books 17–21)

Meet the Author

https://www.LAMoeszinger.com

Meet the Publisher, Urban Chronicles Publishing House

https://www.NewYouniversityChronicles.com

Step into the whirlwind world of New York's glitzy underbelly, where the scintillating secrets and laugh-out-loud confessions of a metropolitan woman are laid bare by someone truly in the know. Through essays pulled from her chic "Manhattanite's Survival Guide—Success in the City," L invites us on an unforgettable strut from her glamorous youth, through her middle-aged mazes, and into her fabulous sixties.

For the juiciest tidbits about L's life, her "Manhattan Chronicles" blog is the place to be. This blog is an unfiltered dive into L's world, from her spiritual musings to her meticulous weigh-ins to her New Youniversity Chronicles—The Manhattan Diaries series—personal tales. Dive into her cosmos at her blog site: https://www.ManhattanChronicles.com.

The Manhattan Diaries Series

Unlock Manhattan
Master the Art of Lasting Impressions

Manhattan Allure
Just Like That

Introduction: Lights, City, Action~ Manhattan's Manual to Magnetism and Memory!

Hey there, urban explorers! As you stride through the dazzling lights of the city that never sleeps, do you ever find yourself wondering about the secrets hidden behind the velvet ropes of glamour and style? Does this bustling energy of New York fill you with confidence, or are you still on a journey to discover the secrets that set the city's elite apart when it comes to leaving unforgettable impressions? Well, darlings, it's time to step into the spotlight because the brilliance of your future should always outshine the sparkle of your past. And guess what? I've got more than just a glimpse to offer. Welcome to The Manhattan Diaries debut—"Unlock Manhattan: Master the Art of Lasting Impressions."

In this enchanting journey, I'm going to whisk you behind the scenes of the city's elite. You see, success in the city isn't just about wit or mastering the chic streets—it's about making a lasting impression at every swanky event, from uptown soirees to downtown extravaganzas. I've rubbed shoulders with the glitterati, sipped cocktails at the trendiest spots, and uncovered the secrets that keep NYC's finest leaving their mark. But, my dears, remember this: True charm always starts from within.

Imagine this as your VIP ticket to a luxury, limited-edition of The Manhattan Diaries series, experience. Whether you choose to savor it over leisurely days, indulge week by week, or sip cocktails on Manhattan's breathtaking rooftops while flipping through the pages, the pace is entirely yours. Picture yourself delving into a chapter with your morning latte or conquering the entire book during a weekend getaway. Within these pages, you'll discover the keys to unlocking a new refined version of yourself, and the magnetism that follows will leave you astounded.

UNLOCK MANHATTAN

As we journey through these pages together, I'll be your confidante, revealing how effortlessly you can conquer the concrete jungle and make those lasting impressions that truly count. This guide isn't just about first impression tips; it's a rebirth of your spirit, your relationships, and your aspirations in the city. Join me in uncovering the secrets that will make you shine as brightly as the city skyline. I'm not just committed to helping you rise among the city's elite; I'm here to ignite the fire in your heart that propels you to your most spectacular self. Embrace it, and the energy of New York will be yours to command!

My passion for this city-centric guide stems from my own personal journey, full of highs and lows, passion, and heartbreaks. Like many city dwellers, I had to forge my own path, sometimes veering off the beaten track. But today, I stand here, ready to inspire you to encounter your city, too, cocktail in hand.

As time sails on the Hudson River, our diverse life paths eventually intersect. For me, the whirlwind of career pursuits, downtown soirees, and self-discovery converged with my love for the city, leading me to work with the Urban Chronicles Publishing House.

Remember, darlings, New York City isn't exclusive to celebrities or trust fund beneficiaries; it's yours too, whether you're in your chic twenties or your sophisticated sixties and beyond. Embrace this journey with me as we embark on a path to city stardom in this first step—The Manhattan Diaries series is a twenty-one step journey; twenty-one books to reinvent and discover a side of you Manhattan's never met.

"Unlock Manhattan" equips you with the tools to not only dream big but to seize those dreams. Pamper your soul with the city's finest, and watch as your dream job, penthouse, or perfect partner follows suit. If you've got city-sized dreams, this series is your golden key! I've seen friends rise to city stardom time and time again, providing that as you align within, the city will reflect it back in glitz and glamour. That's a promise straight from the heart of New York.

Relying on The Manhattan Diaries series has always been my go-to source. Whenever the city threw a curveball my way, this series navigated me right back to my radiant path. The allure of always being on top keeps me returning to these pages, and trust me, it's far more exhilarating than settling for mediocrity.

With each page you turn, you'll discover the blueprint, insider secrets, and the support you need to make your city journey a thrilling adventure. This series is tailored for everyone, from the ambitious career seekers to the social butterflies and empire builders.

There are countless ways to rise in the Big Apple, but if you're searching for the chicest route, it's right here in The Manhattan Diaries. Immerse yourself in its delights while reciting positive mantras, and let the city's vibrancy chase away any doubts; and, in this case, allowing your city star to shine. To truly reign, sometimes we need to shed our old sequins and embrace our radiant selves.

Navigating the City with The Manhattan Diaries

Darlings, welcome to The Manhattan Diaries, the kind of chronicles even Carrie would envy. As the city unfolds its secrets, think of this edition, "Unlock Manhattan: Master the Art of Lasting Impressions," as your very own cosmopolitan diary, as interactive as a VIP pass to New York's top clubs. Each chapter is enriched with journal pages, waiting for your Manhattan musings and anecdotes. Whether you want to record the day's chic highlights in your city beats or delve into deep reflections in your city confessions, these journal pages are yours to fill; also see Cocktails and Chronicles: "Journal Pages: Pen Your Tales" at the end of the book to record even more details.

But . . .

1   Before you start jotting down your thoughts, take a moment to breathe. Close your eyes, and in that quiet moment, whisper a heartfelt "thank you" to the city that never sleeps. Feel that rush of gratitude, as if you've just scored front row tickets to New York Fashion Week. Let that "thank you" resonate deep within your heart—because that, my friends, is the magic of Manhattan.

2   Begin by detailing the fabulous strides you've made since reading the last glamorous advice. Write them down under "Your Triumphs," and bask in the Fifth Avenue feeling that washes over you.

3   Once you've celebrated your triumphs, turn the page to "Your Goals" and script your aspirations. Reflect on what's left to conquer in your metropolitan journey, capturing your next steps in this transformational saga.

Throughout The Manhattan Diaries series, you'll also find timeless "inspirational quotes" that are as iconic as the Empire State Building itself. Think of them as your cosmopolitan compass, guiding your city journey. Relish them like sips from a crystal glass at a swanky Manhattan penthouse party, and let them resonate deep within your urban soul.

As you approach the end of each guide, you'll discover a "City Roundup." Here, you'll find a chic recap summarizing all the insider tips from your city escapades, ensuring you never miss a New York allure minute.

So, get ready to peel back the curtain on NYC's best-kept secrets to making lasting impressions, darlings. Behind the curtain awaits a world of glamour, style, and endless possibilities. It's time to shine brighter than the city lights.

INTRODUCTION—LIGHTS, CITY, ACTION

Unlock Manhattan: Master the Art of Lasting Impressions

Hold tight, darlings of the dazzling city, as we embark on the premier escapade of The Manhattan Diaries: "Unlock Manhattan: Master the Art of Lasting Impressions."

New York City, where a whisper can become a roar and where every glance can be a story waiting to unfold. Here, in the urban jungle where dreams are made and destinies are defined in flashbulb moments, knowing how to stand out isn't a luxury—it's an art.

Imagine this: With the intoxicating aroma of Central Park blossoms wafting by; you make your entrance into a lavish Fifth Avenue soiree. Before you even utter a word, the room is spellbound, hanging onto the promise of your every gesture. That, my love, is the power of a true Manhattanite.

But how, you wonder, does one achieve such urban allure? It's beyond just impeccable taste or the highest heels. It's mastering the rhythm of the city, the spark in your eye, the confidence in your stride. It's knowing when to speak, when to listen, and always leaving them wanting more.

So let's dive deep into the heart of the city that never sleeps, and discover together the secrets of making not just an entrance, but a lasting impression. Because, sweetheart, in the world's most mesmerizing metropolis, it's not just about being seen—it's about being remembered. Prepare for your close-up, and let the city's magic begin!

Meet the Maestros Behind the Curtain

Welcome to the glittering realm of The Manhattan Diaries series, penned by an eclectic group of scribes who know how to make words shimmer just like that Midtown skyline. Each of these writers possesses the kind of Manhattan moxie that's as electrifying as a Saturday night at Studio 54. Picture the literary equivalent of the fabulous foursome from "Sex and the City," but with a little extra Manhattan mascara.

Our authors, darlings, aren't just writers; they're connoisseurs of all things NYC, dishing out stories with the precision of a Fifth Avenue stylist crafting the perfect blowout. Their tales are imbued with the kind of insider knowledge only those who've sipped martinis at the city's most secretive spots can truly understand.

So, as you delve into the pages of The Manhattan Diaries know that you're not just reading words, you're sipping on the prose of New York's finest literary mixologists. Here's to a journey as sparkling and unforgettable as a New York night out. Cheers, darling!

Behind the Scenes with Urban Chronicles Publishing House

In the whirlwind of New York's high society, the Urban Chronicles Publishing House has emerged as the ultimate style sage for modern-day self-help. Over a cosmopolitan-fueled decade, they've become the city's go-to curators for crafting that sought-after, enviable life. The Manhattan Diaries? Envision it as your exclusive, VIP backstage pass, dripping with Upper East Side allure.

If you've ever pictured yourself sashaying through Manhattan with poise, if you've craved that skyline backdrop to your impeccable life, or if you simply seek the secrets whispered in the plush corners of the city's most exclusive clubs—The Manhattan Diaries is your ticket. Crafted under the elite banner, Urban Chronicles Publishing House, this imprint doesn't just offer you insights; it's your personal invite to the city's most glamorous circles.

- ➤ **Forever en Vogue**. Everyone, from the Wall Street moguls to the aspiring Broadway stars, dreams of basking in New York's radiant glow of living a life drenched in style and substance. The wisdom in The Manhattan Diaries is as timeless as a Fifth Avenue romance, ensuring you're always en vogue.

➢ **A Blueprint for the Elite**. Nestled within these pages are the golden rules of city living, from mastering the cocktail chatter to undergoing a dazzling reinvention. Whether you're a seasoned socialite, an ambitious parent, or a fresh-eyed dreamer, these guides have something to make your heart race a little faster.

➢ **The Perfect Accessory**. Their petite stature makes these guides a seamless fit for your Prada clutch or your gym tote. Think of them as your urban survival kit—a blend of wisdom and wit that's as crucial as your red lipstick for those Manhattan nights.

Take a sip of this rich concoction, and let the Urban Chronicles Publishing House unlock Manhattan, unveiling a New York you only dreamed of. Welcome to the allure of the elite, darling.

Unveiling The Ridge Publishing Group

Picture The Ridge Publishing Group as the rising star on New York's literary and entertainment horizon. Envision an eclectic empire—books, cinema, and board games—setting the stage to become the world's haute couture of theological discourse. Think Broadway and Avenues of the Americas for publishing resources: luxurious, elite, and unparalleled.

Dive into their esteemed collections. They hold the keys to the illustrious Guardians of Biblical Truth Publishing Group and the evocative New Narrated Study Bible (NNSB) series. Delve deeper and find the Hoyle Theology Publishing Group and its opulent Hoyle Theology Encyclopedia— a treasure trove for the cerebral sophisticate. And for those who like their theology paired with a cinematic flair, there's the Documentaries in Print Publishing Group with its tantalizing series like Defending the Faith. And, of course, for those cocktail nights with a side of divine strategy, the Heaven's Seminary board games and card decks offer a chic twist.

But that's not all. The Ridge Publishing Group is more than a theological publishing powerhouse; it's a brand. Alongside its flagship, it flaunts trendy imprints: AuthorsDoor Group and AuthorsDoor Leadership (check them out at the glamorous digital boulevard of https://www.AuthorsDoor.com), the ritzy Urban Chronicles Publishing House and New Youniversity (make your reservation at https://www.NewYouniversityChronicles.com), and the novel delights of Ethan Fox Books (sip your martini and browse https://www.EthanFoxBooks.com).

For a sneak peek into the world where theology meets Manhattan glamour, rendezvous at their digital penthouse: https://www.Ridge PublishingGroup.com. It's theology made chic.

A NOTE TO THE READER

Typos in this book? Errors (and inconsistencies) can get through proofreaders, so if you do find any typos or grammatical errors in this book, I'd be very grateful if you could let me know using this email address typos@LAMoeszinger.com. Thank you ☺

A Stride On the Wild Side: Perfecting the Manhattan Walk of Fame

Manhattan, a city where dreams aren't just dreamed—they're walked. Every inch, from the tip of Battery Park to the upper echelons of Harlem, reverberates with the rhythms of footsteps, each telling a unique story of ambition, romance, and undying spirit. This isn't just any city; it's a theatre where the streets are stages, and your walk, darling, is the star performance.

Now imagine: The sun is setting, casting a golden hue over the city, and you're on the cusp of Central Park, poised to make your descent into the buzzing heart of Midtown. Heads turn, not because of the designer shoes gracing your feet, but the power and intent with which you command the pavement. That, darling, is taking A Stride On the Wild Side—an art form that speaks of confidence, charm, and a hint of wild abandon.

In this intoxicating chapter of The Manhattan Diaries, we'll delve deep into the magnetic walk, which leaves a trail of whispers and gasps in its wake. Whether it's the audacious stomp that says "I own this town" or the sultry sway of someone who knows all the city's secrets, each step can be a statement, and I'm here to help you craft yours. But remember, the Manhattan Walk of Fame isn't just about the tilt of the hip or the rhythm of the feet. It's an ode to the city itself—a harmonious blend of the classic and the contemporary, the gritty and the glamorous. It's walking with the wisdom of those who walked before you and the audacity of those who'll follow.

So, come with me, as we trace the steps of icons, learning the moves that made them legendary. We'll dance with the shadows of the brownstones and waltz with the reflections in the glass skyscrapers. Because, sweetheart, in this city of dreams, it's not just about where you're going, but how you get there. Prepare to turn the sidewalk into your runway, for Manhattan is ready for your encore. Welcome to The Manhattan Diaries—where your every step can steal the spotlight.

Mastering the Manhattan Rhythm

In the ever-pulsating heart of Manhattan, where the streets hum with a rhythm as distinct as the city itself, "Mastering the Manhattan Rhythm is about syncing your stride to the city's heartbeat. It's not just walking; it's embracing the cadence of a city that never pauses, a city that dances to the beat of ambition, dreams, and endless possibilities.

➢ **The Symphony of the Streets**. As you step onto the bustling sidewalks, become a part of Manhattan's symphony. It's a rhythm set by the clatter of subway grates, the melody of street musicians, and the tempo of hurried footsteps. Your walk becomes a note in this urban symphony, a harmony with the city's dynamic soundtrack.

➢ **Adapting to the Neighborhood's Tempo**. Each neighborhood in Manhattan has its unique tempo. The brisk, assertive steps of the Financial District, the leisurely, thoughtful stroll of the Upper West Side, the energetic, vibrant strut of Times Square. Mastering the Manhattan rhythm is about adapting your pace, your energy to match the neighborhood's spirit.

➢ **The Ballet of Dodging and Weaving**. In a city that's always in motion, your walk is a ballet of dodging and weaving. It's about navigating through the crowds with grace and agility, a dance that requires poise, alertness, and a touch of audacity. It's a skill that says you're not just in the city; you're a part of it.

➢ **The Confidence in Every Step**. But the true secret to mastering the Manhattan rhythm? Confidence. Walk with a purpose, as if every street is your runway, every crosswalk a spotlight. It's the confidence that tells the world you're not just passing through; you own these streets, you belong to this city.

➢ **The Flair of the Fashionable Stride**. In Manhattan, fashion and walking style are intertwined. It's about how your shoes click against the concrete, how your coat sways with each step, how your accessories add rhythm to your movement. This flair is your personal signature, a visual rhythm that complements the city's vibe.

➢ **The Art of Pausing**. Just as important as your walk is the art of the pause. In a city that's always rushing, a well-timed pause—to admire a street performer, gaze at a storefront, or simply take in the skyline—is a note of stillness in the symphony of motion, a reminder to appreciate the city's beauty amidst the hustle.

➢ **The Syncopation of Crosswalks**. The crosswalks of Manhattan are stages for a momentary performance. Here, your walk is syncopated with the traffic lights, a rhythmic dance with fellow pedestrians, a shared moment of movement where for a brief time, your paths intersect and your rhythms align.

➢ **Navigating the Crowds with Grace**. Mastering the Manhattan rhythm means navigating the crowds with grace and courtesy. It's about moving through the masses with ease, an effortless flow that respects the pace and space of those around you, a dance of mutual understanding in a crowded ballroom.

➢ **The Sunset Stride**. As the day wanes, embrace the sunset stride. This is a time when the city transitions from day to night, and your walk reflects this change—slower, more contemplative, a rhythmic reflection of the day's end and the night's promise.

In Mastering the Manhattan Rhythm, it's about more than just keeping pace; it's about moving in sync with the city's soul. It's a celebration of the dance of life that happens on these streets every day, a dance you're now a part of. So put on your best shoes, darling, and step out into the rhythm of Manhattan, where every step is a declaration of your love affair with the city.

Your Triumphs: City Runways Activities

Inspirational Quote

IF PEOPLE LIKE YOU, THEY WILL LISTEN TO YOU, BUT IF THEY TRUST YOU, THEY'LL DO BUSINESS WITH YOU. — Zig Ziglar

Your Goals: Intentions and Thoughts

The Confidence in Your Stride

In the dazzling drama that is Manhattan, where every sidewalk is a stage and every passerby an audience, The Confidence in Your Stride is about owning your path with a boldness that's as captivating as the city itself. It's not just the rhythm of your steps; it's the assurance in each stride, the unwritten story of self-assurance that you narrate with every move you make.

➢ **The Strut of Self-Assurance**. Imagine walking down Fifth Avenue, each step a declaration of your presence. This isn't just walking; it's strutting—a stride that speaks volumes of your self-assurance. It's the kind of walk that turns the city's sidewalks into your personal runway, where confidence is your most cherished accessory.

➢ **The Poise in the Pavement Dance**. In the dance of the Manhattan pavement, your poise is key. It's in the way you navigate the bustling crowds, your head held high, your gaze steadfast. This poise isn't just physical; it's an attitude, a state of mind that says, "I am in control, I am undaunted."

➢ **The Boldness of Being Unapologetically You**. Your stride is a bold statement of being unapologetically you. In a city teeming with millions, your walk sets you apart. It's the way you embrace your unique style, your individuality, striding not just to fit in, but to stand out, to be remembered.

➢ **The Rhythm of Resilience**. Each step is a rhythm of resilience. It's about walking through the city as if you've conquered it, as if each street corner holds a story of your triumphs. This resilience is the pulse in your step, a cadence that resonates with the city's own spirit of never backing down.

➢ **The Elegance of Effortlessness**. And yet, in all this, there's an elegance of effortlessness. It's a subtle grace, an ease that suggests that no matter how fast the city moves, you're moving with it, not against it. Your stride is as fluid as the East River, as graceful as the arches of the Brooklyn Bridge.

➤ **The Harmony of Heels on Cobblestone**. There's a unique music to be found in the click of heels on Manhattan's cobblestone streets. It's a harmony that signifies confidence, an audible signature of your presence. Whether you're navigating the historic streets of the Meatpacking District or the charm of Greenwich Village, your heels sing a song of self-assured elegance.

➤ **The Power of the Posture**. Your stride isn't just about the steps you take; it's also about your posture. Standing tall, shoulders back, chin up—it's a physical manifestation of confidence. In Manhattan, where the skyscrapers reach for the stars, your posture should reflect the same ambition, a visual echo of the city's upward aspirations.

➤ **The Cadence of Confidence and Clam**. In a city that thrives on energy, there's confidence in displaying calm within the chaos. Your stride should have a tempo that marries confidence with composure, a pace that says you're unflustered by the city's frenzy, moving through it with a serenity that's as striking as it is rare.

➤ **The Magnetism of the Measured Stride**. There's a magnetism in a measured stride, a deliberate pacing that draws the eye. It's about knowing that confidence isn't always in speed; sometimes, it's in the deliberate, thoughtful pace at which you engage with the world around you, a stride that invites admiration and respect.

In The Confidence in Your Stride, it's about embodying the essence of Manhattan—bold, unyielding, and utterly dazzling. It's about understanding that in this city, the way you walk can speak louder than words, can tell a story more captivating than any penned novel. So, darling, let your steps be your narrative, your stride your legacy in the city of dreams.

Your Triumphs: Stride and Confidence Activities

A STRIDE ON THE WILD SIDE

Your Goals: Intentions and Thoughts

The Dance of Diversity

In the kaleidoscopic whirl of Manhattan, where every street corner is a crossroad of cultures and every face tells a different story, The Dance of Diversity is about embracing the myriad rhythms that make up the city's heart. It's a dance of steps as varied and vibrant as Manhattan itself. A celebration of the countless styles that parade the pavements.

- ➤ **A Melting Pot of Movements**. On these streets, your walk is part of a greater tapestry—a melting pot of movements. Here, the poised, elegant strides of the Upper East Side mingle with the energetic, bouncy steps of East Village artists. Each style is a reflection of the city's diverse personalities, a physical manifestation of the myriad lives that pulse through these streets.

- ➤ **The Eclectic Stride Symphony**. The beauty of Manhattan's walk lies in its eclectic nature. It's where the confident, long stride of a Broadway star contrast with the hurried, zigzagging rush of a Wall Street banker. This diversity creates a symphony of strides, a visual representation of the city's multifaceted soul.

- ➤ **Stepping to the Beat of Different Drums**. In The Dance of Diversity, it's about stepping to the beat of different drums. It's rhythm that changes from block to block—from the salsa steps in Washington Heights to the smooth, jazz-like saunter in Harlem. Each neighborhood brings its own beat, and your walk adapts, a chameleon of rhythm.

- ➤ **A Celebration of Individuality**. Above all, this dance is a celebration of individuality. In a city that champions self-expression, your walk is your personal signature—as unique as your fingerprint. It's about owning your stride, whether it's a carefree amble or a purposeful march, and knowing that in Manhattan, every step is accepted, celebrated, cherished.

- ➤ **The Rhythm of Resilience**. In this dance, every step also speaks to the resilience of the city and its inhabitants. The determined march of an aspiring actress, the steady gait of a long-time local, or the eager stride of a recent arrival—each reflects the enduring spirit of Manhattan, a city built on dreams, grit, and an unyielding zest for life.

- ➤ **The Fusion of Fashion and Footsteps**. The dance of diversity is not just in the steps but also in the fashion that adorns them. The eclectic mix of styles—from designer heels tapping down Fifth Avenue to vintage sneakers pounding the pavements of Brooklyn—is a visual feast, a testament to the city's role as a global fashion capital.

- ➤ **The Choreography of Chance Encounters**. Manhattan's sidewalks are stages for chance encounters, where diverse paths cross and new stories begin. It's in these spontaneous moments—a shared smile, a brief conversation—that the city's dance becomes a communal experience, a shared rhythm that binds strangers in the briefest yet most profound ways.

- ➤ **The Unity in Diversity**. Lastly, The Dance of Diversity is a reminder of the unity in diversity. In the shared streets of Manhattan, these different walks, these different rhythms, come together in a harmonious coexistence. It's a beautiful, chaotic dance where every different step, every unique stride, plays a part in the grand performance of the city.

In The Dance of Diversity, your walk is more than just a way to get from one place to another; it's an integral part of the city's fabric, a contribution to the rich, vibrant story that is Manhattan. So take to the streets, darling, and let your walk be your own—a dance step in the never-ending ballet of the city that always dances.

Your Triumphs: Dance of Diversity Activities

Inspirational Quote

NEVER BEND YOUR HEAD. ALWAYS HOLD IT HIGH. LOOK THE WORLD STRAIGHT IN THE EYE. — Helen Keller

Your Goals: Intentions and Thoughts

Leaving a Lasting Impression

In the glittering carousel that is Manhattan, where every interaction is a chance to sparkle, Leaving a Lasting Impression is about making sure your presence is felt long after you've glided out of the room. It's the art of imprinting yourself in the memories of those you meet, a lingering essence that's as indelible as the city's skyline.

➤ **The Sparkle of a Memorable Conversation**. Your words should be like jewels—bright, captivating, unforgettable. It's about engaging in conversations that leave a mark, where your wit, charm, and insight linger in the air like the afterglow of a dazzling party. Whether it's a clever quip, a thoughtful observation, or a shared laugh, make every word count.

➤ **The Signature Style that Speaks Volumes**. In Manhattan, your style is your signature—make it bold, make it unique, make it you. Whether it's a statement piece that turns heads or a subtle nod to the latest trends, dress in a way that leaves a visual imprint, a style that's remembered long after you've left the scene.

➤ **The Art of the Graceful Exit**. There's a finesse to exiting gracefully, a way of leaving that keeps them wanting more. It's about making your departure as memorable as your entrance—a warm smile, a final wave, a look that promises more tales to come. Leave them with the feeling that the night is lesser without you.

➤ **The Power of a Personal Connection**. In a city of millions, personal connections are precious. Make each interaction count by being genuinely interested, by making people feel seen and heard. It's these connections that resonate, that turn a fleeting meeting into a lasting memory.

➢ **The Echo of Your Enthusiasm**. Let your enthusiasm be contagious, a spark that ignites interest and admiration. Be passionate about your interests, your dreams, your conversations. This energy is magnetic, leaving a powerful imprint.

➢ **The Allure of Mystery**. In a city where everyone is trying to stand out, sometimes the most unforgettable impression is one shrouded in mystery. Leave them with a hint of intrigue, an unsolved riddle about who you are. It's the stories untold and the secrets just hinted at that often linger longest in the mind.

➢ **The Resonance of Genuine Emotion**. Emotions resonate. When you express genuine joy, sincere interest, or heartfelt concern, it leaves a deep impression. In Manhattan's whirlwind of superficial encounters, authentic emotions stand out like beacons, memorable for their rarity and depth.

➢ **The Personal Touch in Farewells**. Make your goodbyes personal. A personalized complement, a reference to a shared moment, or a thoughtful parting remark shows that you were truly present in the interaction, making your departure a meaningful moment rather than a mere formality.

➢ **The Digital Footprint**. Leaving a lasting impression can also extend to your digital presence. A thoughtful message, a well-timed comment, or a shared link to something discussed in person can reinforce and enhance the memory of your physical interactions.

In Leaving a Lasting Impression, it's about understanding that in the grand tapestry of Manhattan, you are a vivid thread, weaving your own unique pattern. It's about ensuring that your presence is a melody that lingers, a perfume that haunts, a touch that's felt long after it's gone. In this city of fleeting moments and endless encounters, leave a part of yourself in every step, every word, every glance—and become a lasting part of its infinite story.

Your Triumphs: Lasting Impressions Activities

Inspirational Quote

BRANDING DEMANDS COMMITMENT; COMMITMENT TO CONTINUAL RE-INVENTION, STRIKING CHORDS WITH PEOPLE TO STIR THEIR EMOTIONS, AND COMMITMENT TO IMAGINATION. IT IS EASY TO BE CYNICAL ABOUT SUCH THINGS, MUCH HARDER TO BE SUCCESSFUL. — Sir Richard Branson

Your Goals: Intentions and Thoughts

Your Goals: Intentions and Thoughts

Dressed to Distill:
Crafting an Ensemble that Whispers Legends

Manhattan, a city where tales are woven into the very fabric of its streets. Where every whispered legend and every roaring scandal is not just in the words spoken, but in the outfits that tell their own story. Here it's not just about the threads you wear, but the tales they tell.

Envision this: A midsummer evening in Tribeca, where the setting sun paints golden hues, and there you are, draped in an ensemble that doesn't just fit, but feels. It's not about the brand or the trend, but the aura, the allure, the story whispered through every stitch. That, darling, is the essence of Dressed to Distill.

In this glamorous chapter of The Manhattan Diaries, we delve deep into the wardrobe of Manhattan's elite, not to dissect brands, but to distill legends. From the enigmatic little black dress with a history as rich as its hue, to the rebellious leather jacket that's seen more adventures than most, every piece has a story to tell. But this isn't merely about fabric—it's far more intimate. It's about crafting an identity, weaving tales of passion, intrigue, and ambition into every outfit. It's about understanding that in Manhattan, an ensemble isn't just clothing—it's a prologue.

Join me, as we sift through the closets of Manhattan's most iconic, to discover not just outfits, but legacies. Understand the power of a well-tailored suit, the mystery of a flowing scarf, and the bold statement of red heels on a rainy day. Let's embark on a journey where you don't just dress to impress, but dress to distill. Where every thread, every accessory, every color choice becomes a testament to who you are and the legends you wish to weave.

Welcome to The Manhattan Diaries—where fashion isn't just about style; it's about stories. So, darling, are you ready to dress not just for the day, but for the tales you wish to tell? After all, in Manhattan, every outfit is an opportunity to become legendary.

The Whisper of Fabric and Folklore

In the intricate tapestry of Manhattan, where every thread has a tale and every garment a ghost of the past, The Whisper of Fabric and Folklore is about draping yourself in more than just clothes—it's about adorning yourself in the city's history. Each piece in your wardrobe is not merely a fashion choice; it's a whisper from the past, a fragment of a story waiting to be told.

➤ **Vintage Tales Told Anew**. Imagine slipping into a '50s vintage dress from a boutique in Chelsea. It's not just silk and stitches; it's a time capsule, an echo of the laughter and secrets of Manhattan's past. With each swish of the skirt, you're not just walking; you're transporting history into the present, letting the tales woven into the fabric come alive.

➤ **The Legacy in Lace and Linen**. Every lace trim, every linen skirt carries the legacy of its makers and wearers. Wearing them is like tracing the outline of a bygone era—the delicate craftsmanship of the lace speaks of old-world elegance, while the linen whispers of summer days spent in Central Park, of artist capturing the city's spirit.

➤ **The Romance of Rescued Relics**. There's a romance in wearing rescued relics—a hat from a decades-old haberdashery, a brooch from a long-closed Upper East Side jewelry store. Each piece is a character in Manhattan's ongoing narrative, a relic that adds depth and texture to your personal story.

➤ **The Echoes of Iconic Eras**. In the folds of a flapper dress or the cut of a classic trench, the echoes of iconic Manhattan eras live on. To wear these pieces is to carry the legacy of the city's history, to be a moving homage to the styles and stories that have shaped Manhattan.

> **The Ballads in Buttons and Beads**. Each button and bead on your attire sings a ballad of its own. It might be the intricate button from a '20s speakeasy coat, each press a whisper of jazz and gin, or the beads of a Roaring Twenties flapper dress, echoing the laughter and liberation of an era. These small details are not just adornments; they're minuscule maestros of history's orchestra.

> **The Storytelling of Scarves and Shawls**. Wrap yourself in the storytelling of scarves and shawls, each a canvas of color and culture. Perhaps it's a silk scarf from a bygone luxury brand, its patterns narrating tales of old Manhattan glamour, or a hand-woven shawl from a Lower East Side artisan, echoing the city's rich tapestry of immigrant stories.

> **The Chronicles of Couture**. High fashion pieces are not just about luxury; they're chronicles in couture. A designer gown or a bespoke suit from a renowned Manhattan tailor is a chapter of craftsmanship and creativity, a testament to the city's enduring influence on global fashion trends and its role in sculpting the narrative of haute couture.

> **The Folklore in Footwear**. Even your footwear carries folklore. The vintage boots sourced from a Greenwich Village thrift store have walked the city's historic streets, each scuff a mark of Manhattan's ever-evolving story, while designer heels from a Fifth Avenue boutique whisper of modern-day fairy tales, of aspirations and achievements.

In The Whisper of Fabric and Folklore, your wardrobe becomes a gateway to the past, a collection of stories that you bring to life with every step. It's about recognizing that in Manhattan, fashion is a dialogue with history, a love affair with the past. So, darling, as you dress, listen to the whispers of the city—in every seam, there's a story, in every thread, a legend.

Your Triumphs: Fabric Chronicles Activities

Inspirational Quote

IF YOU LOOK AT WHAT YOU HAVE IN LIFE, YOU'LL ALWAYS HAVE MORE.
— Oprah Winfrey

DRESSED TO DISTILL

Your Goals: Intentions and Thoughts

Symbolism in Silhouette and Shade

In the vibrant mosaic that is Manhattan, where every color tells a tale and every silhouette sings a song, Symbolism in Silhouette and Shade is a dive into the deeper meanings behind the hues and contours we drape ourselves in. It's about understanding that in this city, your outfit is a canvas, and every choice of color and cut is a stroke of your personal story.

➤ **The Power of Color**. In the spectrum of Manhattan's fashion, each color resonates with its own symbolism. The daring red of a cocktail dress whispers tales of passion and ambition, the cool blue of a summer blouse sings of calm and clarity, and the timeless black of an evening gown echoes with sophistication and mystery. It's about choosing hues that not only complement your complexion but also your character.

➤ **Silhouettes that Speak Volumes**. The silhouette of your attire is a visual narrative. The sharp lines of a tailored blazer tell a story of precision and professionalism, while the flowing grace of a maxi dress hums a melody of freedom and creativity. In Manhattan, the shape of your clothes is a reflection of your personal journey, an outline of your individuality.

➤ **Shades of History and Heritage**. Every shade you wear is imbued with history and heritage. It's the deep green that harks back to the lush parks at the heart of the city, the vibrant neons that echo the electric energy of Times Square, the muted tones that reflect the historic brownstones of Brooklyn. Your palette is a homage to the city and its rich tapestry of stories.

➤ **The Contrast of Light and Dark**. Play with the contrast of light and dark in your wardrobe to mirror the dynamic duality of Manhattan. The interplay of light and shadow in your outfit can symbolize the city's juxtapositions—the classic and the modern, the hustle and the tranquility, the dreams and the realities.

> **Echoing the Seasons in Shades**. Let your wardrobe echo the seasons of Manhattan. The blooming pinks and soft pastels of spring, the bold and bright hues of summer, the earthly tones of fall, and the stark, crisp colors of winter—each season brings its own palette, a cyclic rhythm of life in the city.

> **The Whisper of White and the Tales of Black**. In Manhattan's wardrobe, white and black tell their own timeless tales. The crispness of white, from elegant blouses to summer dresses, speaks of new beginnings and endless possibilities, a blank page in the city's diary. Black, on the other hand, is the color of the Manhattan night— sophisticated, mysterious, a symbol of the city's never-ending allure and depth.

> **The Metaphor in Metallics**. Metallic tones in your wardrobe are not just glam; they're a metaphor for the city itself. The shimmer of gold, the shine of silver, the glint of bronze—each reflects the city's dazzling ambitions and dreams, its status as a beacon for those seeking their own golden opportunities. Wearing metallics is like donning a piece of the city's spirit, a wearable symbol of Manhattan's magnetic allure.

In Symbolism in Silhouette and Shade, dressing becomes a form of expression, a way to tell your story through the colors you wear and the lines you choose. It's about understanding that in Manhattan, fashion is more than skin-deep—it's a language of its own, a way to communicate who you are and the tales you carry. So, as you select your ensemble, remember that you're painting a picture, not just on your body, but on the canvas of the city.

Your Triumphs: Silhouette and Shade Activities

Your Goals: Intentions and Thoughts

Accessories as Artifacts of Adventure

In the dazzling drama of Manhattan, where every detail tells a story, Accessories as Artifacts of Adventure is about turning every adornment into a testament of your personal journey. It's the art of choosing accessories that are not mere embellishments, but narrators of your life's most thrilling tales.

- ➤ **The Charisma of the Cherished Keepsake**. Think of the vintage brooch you picked up at a quaint shop in the West Village or the delicate locket inherited from a glamorous great-aunt. These are not just accessories; they are cherished keepsakes, each with a backstory that adds layers of intrigue and allure to your ensemble. They whisper of past loves, of family history, of adventures long gone but not forgotten.

- ➤ **The Tales Told by Travel Treasures**. Every scarf, bracelet, or hat acquired on your travels is a chapter of your adventures. The silk scarf from Paris, the beaded necklace from Morocco, the handcrafted hat from New Orleans—each piece is a memento of a place, a time, and an experience, a physical reminder of the wide, wild world you've embraced.

- ➤ **The Bold Statement of the Statement Piece**. In the city that never sleeps, a statement piece can speak volumes. It could be the oversized sunglasses that shield you from the city's glare while adding an air of mystery, or the daring pair of heels that tell a story of defiance and confidence. These pieces are your armor and your proclamation, a bold declaration of your presence in the city's endless narrative.

- ➤ **The Whimsy of the Unexpected Find**. There's a special thrill in the unexpected find, the serendipitous discovery of a unique piece that somehow finds its way to you. It could be a quirky thrift store find or a hand-me-down with a history, each with its own quirky tale, adding a touch of whimsy and a dash of destiny to your look.

➤ **The Echoes of Timeless Elegance**. And then, there are the timeless pieces—the classic watch, the elegant pearl earrings, the understated gold chain. These are the accessories that echo timeless elegance, pieces that transcend trends and tell a story of enduring style and grace, a nod to the city's evergreen charm.

➤ **The Romance of Heirloom Jewelry**. There's an undeniable romance in donning heirloom jewelry. The antique ring passed down through generations, the art deco necklace that's seen a century of soirees— these pieces are not just beautiful. They're steeped in history, each stone and setting a witness to the love, laughter, and tears of those who wore them before. Wearing these pieces in Manhattan gives a sense of continuity, a link to the past in the ever-changing cityscape.

➤ **The Signature Piece as a Personal Emblem**. Cultivate the habit of wearing a signature piece—an accessory that becomes synonymous with your persona. It could be a hat, a custom-made pair of boots, or a unique belt buckle. This piece becomes an integral part of your identity, a visual emblem that people associate with your character and story.

➤ **The Whispers of Wanderlust in Worldly Pieces**. Finally, let your accessories reflect your spirit of wanderlust. The Tibetan beads picked up on a trek, the Italian leather satchel from a Florentine market, or the avant-garde hat from a Tokyo boutique—these worldly pieces are whispers of your travels, tangible reminders of your global adventures and the diverse cultures that have touched your life.

In Accessories as Artifacts of Adventure, each accessory you choose is a fragment of your personal legend, a tangible piece of your journey through life and through the streets of Manhattan. It's about curating a collection that's as unique as your story, a wearable diary of where you've been and who you are. So, as you adorn yourself each day, remember, darling, you're not just accessorizing; you're adding chapters to your own epic tales.

Your Triumphs: Stories in Accessories Activities

Inspirational Quote

BELIEVE YOU CAN AND YOU'RE HALFWAY THERE. — Theodore Roosevelt

Your Goals: Intentions and Thoughts

Legacy in Layers

In the ever-evolving tapestry of Manhattan, where styles blend and histories intertwine, Legacy in Layers is about the art of wearing your story through the layers you don. It's a sartorial sonnet to the city's multifaceted nature, where each layer you wear is a verse of your own personal epic.

> ➤ **The Time Traveler's Wardrobe**. Think of layering as time-traveling with fashion. A vintage '40s coat draped over a modern minimalist dress, or a classic '60s blouse paired with contemporary skinny jeans—each combination is a crossing of eras, a dialogue between the past and the present. It's about weaving the threads of different times into a single outfit that speaks of history and modernity in one breath.

> ➤ **The Symphony of Textures and Eras**. In Manhattan, layering is also a symphony of textures and eras. The ruggedness of a leather jacket against the softness of a silk scarf, the crispness of a tailored blazer atop the flow of a bohemian skirt—it's a dance of contrasts, a celebration of diversity. Each texture, each piece from a different era, adds its own tone to the melody of your attire.

> ➤ **The Narrative in Nuances**. Every nuanced layer you add tells a part of your story. The scarf from your travels abroad, the heirloom watch, the ring you bought for yourself on your first big promotion—each layer is a chapter of your life, a tangible representation of your triumphs, travels, and transformations.

> ➤ **The Elegance of Effortless Layering**. The key to mastering legacy in layers is effortless elegance. It's about combining pieces in a way that looks unintentionally intentional, as if each item was casually thrown on but somehow perfectly fits together. It's an art form, a delicate balance between making a statement and whispering a story.

> **The Comfort in Familiar Fibers**. There's a comfort in layering pieces that have journeyed with you through life. The cozy sweater you've curled up in for years, the scarf that's accompanied you on countless autumn strolls through Central Park—these pieces are like old friends, their fibers rich with memories and sentiments. Layering them is a way to surround yourself with the familiar, a sartorial embrace of your personal history.

> **The Drama of Draped Histories**. Embrace the drama in draping histories over your frame. A dramatic cape from a forgotten era, a shawl handed down through generations—these pieces are not just dramatic in their appearance but in the stories they carry. Wearing them is akin to draping yourself in a living, breathing history, a moving tapestry of times gone by.

> **The Whisper of Seasonal Stories**. Each season in Manhattan brings its own narrative, and your layers can reflect this. The light, breezy fabrics of summer tell of sun-soaked days by the Hudson, while the heavy wools of winter whisper of cozy evenings in bustling cafes. Your layers are a response to the city's seasonal stories, a sartorial adaptation to its changing moods.

> **The Personal Archival in Apparel**. Finally, see your layered look as a personal archival in apparel. You're not just wearing clothes; you're curating a collection, showcasing an exhibit of your life. Each layer is a piece of your personal museum, an artifact that represents a facet of your unique journey.

In Legacy in Layers, your fashion is more than just a statement; it's a storytelling device, a way of paying homage to the many layers of your life against the backdrop of Manhattan's ever-changing scene. So, wrap yourself in the layers of your legacy, darling, and walk the streets of Manhattan as a living, breathing narrative of style and substance.

Your Triumphs: Wrapping in Layers Activities

Inspirational Quote

WHEN YOU HAVE A DREAM, YOU'VE GOT TO GRAB IT AND NEVER LET GO.
— Carol Burnett

Your Goals: Intentions and Thoughts

Your Goals: Intentions and Thoughts

3

The Art of Conversation: Mingling with Moxie and Manhattanite Mastery

Manhattan, where skyscrapers touch the heavens and where every rooftop lounge becomes the setting of tales whispered over crystal cocktail glasses. In a city that's always alight with dreamers and doers, it's not just about being in the room; it's about stealing the show with wit, wisdom, and a sprinkle of whimsy.

Now picture this: You're at The Rainbow Room, standing with a martini in hand, and every head turns not because of the sparkle of your jewelry, but the sparkle of your conversation. That, darling, is the Manhattan Art of Mingling, a dance that speaks of curiosity, charisma, and an undeniable connection.

In this intoxicating chapter of The Manhattan Diaries, we'll dive deep into the world of cocktail conversation. From the delicate art of the opener, as tantalizing as the twist in a classic martini, to the depth and nuance of a dialogue, as rich as a vintage Bordeaux, you'll unravel the layers of conversing with style and substance.

But remember, it's not just about words. Oh, no. It's about tuning into the city's undercurrents, about speaking with an intention, a secret, a wish. It's about reading the room, sensing its vibes, and responding with a conversation that's both intimate and universal.

So, come with me, as we weave through the mélange of voices that fill Manhattan's finest establishments, mastering the art of conversation that doesn't just entertain, but captivates. Because, darling, in Manhattan, every dialogue is a dance, every word a step, every pause a beat. Gear up to lead that dance, for the city's most discerning audience is listening. Welcome to The Manhattan Diaries—where your words, like the city's lights, can dazzle and delight.

The Magic of the Opening Line

In the electric air of Manhattan, where every meeting is an opportunity and every conversation a potential masterpiece, The Magic of the Opening Line is about casting a spell with your first words. It's the art of beginning a dialogue with a sparkle that rivals the city lights, an opener that's as inviting as a wink across a crowded room.

- ➢ **The Charisma in the Casual Comment**. Start with the casual yet charismatic comment. It's about finding the extraordinary in the ordinary. Whether it's a playful observation about the weather, a light-hearted remark on the hustle of the city, or a witty comment on the evening's ambiance, your opening line should be an effortless bridge into a deeper conversation.

- ➢ **The Intrigue of the Unexpected Question**. There's a certain intrigue in asking an unexpected, thought-provoking question. It's not the usual "What do you do?" but something more captivating, like "What's the most interesting thing you've seen in Manhattan this week?" It's a question that opens a gateway to stories, inviting a glimpse into the other person's world.

- ➢ **The Flair of Flirting with Culture**. A line that flirts with culture and intellect can be a dazzling opener. Mention a recent exhibit at the Met, a new Broadway show, or a piece of New York history. It shows depth, a shared love for the city's rich cultural tapestry, and an invitation for your companion to share their interests and insights.

- ➢ **The Sparkle of Shared Experiences**. Begin with a line that taps into shared experiences. In a city as dynamic as Manhattan, there's always something to bond over—the latest dining hotspot, the buzz of a new art installation, or the thrill of a Yankees game. It's about creating a sense of camaraderie, a shared thread that can weave you into the fabric of their world.

> **The Allure of Personal Anecdotes**. Infuse your opening line with the allure of a personal anecdote. Share a brief, amusing story from your day or a unique experience you recently had in the city. This approach not only reveals a snippet of your life but also invites the other person to respond with their own tales, fostering a connection built on shared stories.

> **The Wit in Wordplay**. There's an undeniable charm in starting a conversation with a bit of wordplay or a pun, especially if it's relevant to the situation. It demonstrates your linguistic flair and a playful side, setting a light-hearted tone for the conversation that follows.

> **The Mystery of an Open-Ended Statement**. An intriguing, open-ended statement can be a powerful conversation opener. Say something that piques curiosity, like "I just came back from the most unusual place in Manhattan." Such statements invite questions, drawing the listener into a dialogue fueled by their curiosity.

> **The Spark of a Complement**. Begin with a genuine, specific complement. It could be about their outfit, a piece of jewelry, or even their energy. A complement shows attentiveness and appreciation, creating a positive start to the interaction. Just ensure it's sincere and not too personal—a fine balance that resonates well in the sophisticated social landscape of Manhattan.

In The Magic of the Opening Line, it's about wielding your words with the same artistry as Manhattan's skyline—with brilliance, boldness, and a touch of the unexpected. It's about transforming a mere greeting into an enchanting invitation, a doorway into the endless narratives that pulse through the city's veins. So, darling, as you step into your next Manhattan soiree, remember that your opening line is not just a conversation starter, but a spell—one that has the power to captivate and charm, much like the city itself.

Your Triumphs: Conversation Starters Activities

Inspirational Quote

I CAN'T CHANGE THE DIRECTION OF THE WIND, BUT I CAN ADJUST MY
SAILS TO ALWAYS REACH MY DESTINATION. — Jimmy Dean

Your Goals: Intentions and Thoughts

The Dance of Dialogue

In the vibrant ballroom of Manhattan's social scene, where every exchange is a step in an intricate dance, The Dance of Dialogue is about mastering the art of conversation. It's a rhythmic interplay of words and wit, where every back-and-forth is a move in the graceful ballet of banter.

> ➤ **The Choreography of Give and Take**. The essence of the dance is in the give and take. It's not about monopolizing the conversation but about creating a beautiful balance. Like a well-rehearsed dance routine, it involves listening attentively, responding thoughtfully, and allowing the dialogue to flow naturally, each person taking their turn in the spotlight.

> ➤ **The Rhythm of Repartee**. In this dance, timing is key. The rhythm of repartee—that quick, witty, back-and-forth exchange—is the heartbeat of the conversation. It's about being quick on your feet, matching the pace of your partner, and adding your own flair. It's a verbal tango, thrilling and unpredictable.

> ➤ **The Grace of Eloquence**. Eloquence is the grace of this dance. It's about choosing your words for their beauty as well as their meaning, crafting sentences that are not only clear but also captivating. In Manhattan, where style meets substance, eloquence in conversation is as admired as a flawless pirouette.

> ➤ **The Subtlety of Body Language**. Remember, the dance of dialogue isn't just about words; it's also about the subtlety of body language. A tilt of the head, a gentle touch on the arm, a warm smile—these are the unspoken elements of the dance, communicating interest, empathy, and engagement without a single word being spoken.

- ➢ **The Art of the Pivot**. Just like in any dance, knowing how to pivot gracefully is crucial. If the conversation hits a lull or ventures into uncomfortable territory, be ready to pivot smoothly to a new topic, keeping the rhythm of the dialogue alive and the atmosphere light.

- ➢ **Navigating the Nuances of Humor**. Humor is the spark that can ignite the most delightful conversations. It's about knowing how to weave in a joke or a witty remark at just the right moment. But remember, in the dance of Manhattan dialogues, the humor must be tasteful, inclusive, and timely, a delicate feather touch rather than a heavy hand.

- ➢ **The Ebb and Flow of Topics**. A masterful conversation is like a river—it ebbs and flows, meanders and swirls. It's about being adaptable, moving smoothly from lighthearted banter to profound discussion, and back again. This fluidity keeps the dialogue dynamic and engaging, reflecting the ever-changing energy of Manhattan itself.

- ➢ **Active Listening, Active Engaging**. The most crucial step in this dance is active listening. It's about truly hearing what the other person is saying and responding in a way that shows you understand and care. This engagement is what transforms a mere exchange of words into a meaningful dialogue, a true connection that resonates long after the conversation has ended.

In The Dance of Dialogue, conversation is an art form, a delicate balance of listening and speaking, of wit and wisdom. It's about engaging not just with words but with your entire being, creating a connection that transcends the mere exchange of ideas. So, as you step into the whirl of Manhattan's social dance, let your conversations be as enchanting as the city itself—a dance of words, a ballet of banter, a waltz of wordsmithery.

Your Triumphs: Art of Conversation Activities

Inspirational Quote

THE FIRST WORD IN THE PHRASE, "PERSONAL BRAND" IS "PERSONAL." NOW ADD AN "ITY" TO IT, DROP THE "BRAND" AND THAT'S WHAT IT REALLY MEANS. THAT'S THE SECRET. — Adam Ritchie Brand Direction

THE ART OF CONVERSATION

Your Goals: Intentions and Thoughts

Mastering the Art of Subtlety and Suggestion

In the glittering salons and shadowed corners of Manhattan, where every word can be a veiled invitation, Mastering the Art of Subtlety and Suggestion is akin to learning the language of the city itself. It's the skill of weaving hints and implications into your conversation, a delicate dance of words where what's left unsaid can be just as telling as what is spoken.

- ➤ **The Whisper of Implied Meaning**. The beauty of subtlety is in the implied meaning, the art of saying something without really saying it. It's the skill of hinting at an idea, a feeling, or an invitation, leaving enough unsaid to spark the imagination. In a city where directness can sometimes be too blunt, the power lies in suggestion, in the allure of the unspoken.

- ➤ **The Elegance of Euphemism**. Learn the elegance of euphemism and understatement. It's about choosing words that suggest rather than declare, that hint at your intellect and depth without overwhelming. In Manhattan's sophisticated circles, a well-placed euphemism or a clever understatement can be far more impactful than the most flamboyant statement.

- ➤ **The Charm of the Double Entendre**. There's a particular charm in the double entendre, the phrase that dances on the edge of meanings. It's playful, it's provocative, and it's quintessentially Manhattan. It's about engaging your listener in a mental tango, a playful game of verbal cat and mouse that teases the mind and tickles the fancy.

- ➤ **The Intrigue of the Unfinished Thought**. Sometimes, the most powerful part of conversation is the unfinished thought, the trailing sentence that leaves a tantalizing question hanging in the air. This technique creates an aura of mystery and depth, inviting those you converse with to lean in closer, both physically and mentally.

> ➢ **The Sublime Power of the Pause**. And don't forget the power of the pause. A well-timed silence can be as eloquent as the most eloquent speech. In the space between words, there's room for interpretation, for anticipation, for the unspoken words to take root in the listener's mind.

> ➢ **The Delicacy of Diplomacy**. Diplomacy is the essence of subtlety. It's the ability to navigate sensitive topics or divergent opinions with grace and tact. In a city as diverse as Manhattan, mastering the art of diplomatic conversation is essential. It's about expressing your viewpoint in a way that is considerate and respectful, leaving room for different perspectives.

> ➢ **The Intrigue of Indirect Questions**. Asking indirect questions can add an element of intrigue to your conversation. Instead of a straightforward query, frame your questions in a way that invites elaboration, that encourages the other person to reveal more than they might have with a direct approach. It's a subtle way of peeling back layers, revealing the multifaceted nature of your companion.

> ➢ **The Suggestive Power of Metaphors**. Employ metaphors to convey complex ideas or emotions subtly. A well-chosen metaphor can paint a vivid picture, convey a deep emotion, or elucidate a complex idea in a few well-chosen words.

In Mastering the Art of Subtlety and Suggestion, it's about understanding that sometimes, the most memorable conversations are those that leave things unsaid, that hint at hidden depths and unexplored territories. It's about speaking in a way that's as nuanced and layered as the city itself, where every word, every pause, every implication is a brushstroke in the larger painting of your interaction. So, darling, as you navigate the social waters of Manhattan, let your words be as subtly seductive as the city's twinkling skyline—a beacon of intrigue and allure.

Your Triumphs: Subtlety and Suggestion Activities

Inspirational Quote

FOCUS ON IDENTIFYING YOUR TARGET AUDIENCE, COMMUNICATING AN AUTHENTIC MESSAGE THAT THEY WANT AND NEED, AND PROJECT YOURSELF AS AN "EXPERT" WITHIN YOUR NICHE. — Kim Garst

THE ART OF CONVERSATION

Your Goals: Intentions and Thoughts

The Graceful Exit

In the whirlwind of Manhattan's social scene, where every encounter is a performance, The Graceful Exit is the final, defining act. It's about leaving the stage with the same panache with which you entered, ensuring that your departure is as memorable as your arrival. In the city that always watches, how you leave is just as important as how you arrive.

- ➤ **The Art of the Parting Quip**. A well-timed parting quip can be your closing curtain call. It should be light, sparkling, and leave a lingering smile. Think of it as your verbal flourish, a final note that harmonizes the evening's melody, ensuring that your exit is as charming as your entrance.

- ➤ **Leaving Them Wanting More**. The key to a graceful exit is to leave them wanting more. It's about departing at the high point of the conversation, leaving a hint of mystery in the air. Your goodbye should be a promise of future stories, an unspoken agreement that the best is yet to come.

- ➤ **The Elegance of Acknowledgment**. As you make your exit, a nod to your host or a warm acknowledgment of the company you've kept is essential. It's a subtle but significant gesture, a sign of appreciation that adds depth and grace to your departure.

- ➤ **The Poise of the Slow Retreat**. There's a poise in a slow, unhurried retreat. Glide away from the conversation with a calm and collected demeanor. It's not a rush to the door, but a leisurely withdrawal, a sign that while the evening may be ending, the stories and connections will linger.

- ➤ **The Promise in the Glance Back**. As you step away, a glance back can be a powerful tool. It's a silent, but potent message—a look that speaks of connections made, conversations to be continued, and encounters to be repeated. It's a visual bookmark, a reminder that this is not a goodbye, but a pause until the next chapter.

> **The Signature Farewell Gesture**. Cultivate a signature gesture that marks your farewells. Whether it's a gracious wave, a heartwarming smile, or a gentle touch on the shoulder, this personalized gesture becomes your trademark, a memorable flourish that people come to associate with your presence and, just as importantly, your absence.

> **The Art of Leaving at the Right Moment**. Timing is everything in the art of the exit. The perfect moment to leave is when the evening is still vibrant, but before it begins to wane. It's about finding that sweet spot where your departure is noticed, but not disruptive, leaving a space that whispers of your absence.

> **The Subtlety of the Soft Departure**. Sometimes, the most graceful exit is a soft one. It's a departure that's understated, almost unnoticed, like a shadow slipping away at dusk. This subtle exit can be particularly powerful, leaving a gentle but lasting impression of your presence.

> **The Echo of Your Exit in Conversation**. Lastly, leave a conversation or a topic lingering as you exit. It's about making your last words or the subject you were discussing something that continues to resonate, a topic that others will carry on in your absence, keeping the essence of your presence alive even after you've departed.

In The Graceful Exit, it's about ensuring that your departure from any gathering is as impactful as your presence. It's about leaving an imprint of elegance and intrigue, a subtle suggestion that your story within the grand narrative of Manhattan is far from over. So, as you take your leave from the city's glittering nights, do so with the knowledge that your exit is not just an end, but an invitation for future encounters in the city of endless beginnings.

Your Triumphs: Graceful Exits Activities

Inspirational Quote

NO MATTER WHAT YOU'RE GOING THROUGH, THERE'S A LIGHT AT THE END OF THE TUNNEL. — Demi Lovato

THE ART OF CONVERSATION

Your Goals: Intentions and Thoughts

Your Goals: Intentions and Thoughts

4

Eyes that Mesmerize:
The Art of the Gaze In the City's Glare

Manhattan, a city that doesn't just thrive on bustling streets—it thrives on connections, on stolen glances, and on those lingering looks exchanged in its electric glow. In the heart of this urban jungle, it's not just about the strides you make, but the gazes you hold, captivate, and release.

Picture this: You're sipping a cosmopolitan at The Plaza's iconic bar, and though the room brims with tales of old and new, all stories halt when your eyes meet theirs. That, darling, is the power of the Manhattan Gaze—a spell woven not with words, but with irises and intent.

In this intoxicating chapter of The Manhattan Diaries, we'll delve deep into the art of the gaze that transcends the ordinary. From the soft, seductive stare exchanged under the dim light of an Upper East Side soiree to the fierce, fiery look of ambition in a Wall Street boardroom, you'll master the technique to hold, enchant, and mesmerize.

Yet, it's more than mere optics. It's about absorbing the city's soul, mirroring its dreams, desires, and dramas in one's eyes. It's about becoming the silent narrator of the city's unspoken tales, embodying both its glitz and its grit, its dreams and its desolation.

Join me on this sensory journey as we navigate the uncharted terrains of human connection, building bridges with just a look. Unveiling techniques to not just look, but truly see. Because, sweetheart, in Manhattan, every glance is an unspoken story, a secret shared, a bond forged. Ready those lashes and sharpen those stares, for the world is ready to be ensnared by your gaze. Welcome to The Manhattan Diaries—where your eyes can reflect the depth and dazzle of the city's night sky.

The Language of the Look

In the dazzling dance of Manhattan's social labyrinth, where every glance can be a conversation starter, The Language of the Look is about mastering the unspoken dialogues shared through the eyes. It's the art of speaking volumes without uttering a word, a silent symphony played out beneath the city's luminous skyline.

- ➤ **The Flirtatious Flicker**. Begin with the flirtatious flicker, a quick, playful dart of the eyes that says more than any pick-up line ever could. It's the glance you cast across a crowded SoHo gallery or a bustling Midtown bar—a subtle, yet unmistakable signal of interest, a coy invitation to a potential suitor.

- ➤ **The Deep Dive of Intimacy**. Then there's the deep dive—the long, lingering gaze that plunges straight into the soul. In the intimacy of a dimly-lit restaurant or a moonlit walk along the Hudson, this gaze speaks of sincerity and connection, a desire to truly see and be seen. It's the look of understanding, of shared secrets, a bridge built wordlessly between two souls.

- ➤ **The Challenge in the Chorus**. In the boardrooms and the power lunches of Wall Street, your gaze can be a challenge—sharp, unwavering, a testament to your strength and determination. It's a look that asserts your presence, commands respect, and communicates your ambition, as fierce and unflinching as the city itself.

- ➤ **The Compassion in the Glance**. And let's not forget the compassion in a glance—the warm, empathetic eyes that acknowledge a shared struggle or a moment of joy. On the subway, in the streets, in the parks, these looks of compassion weave the fabric of shared humanity, a silent acknowledgment of the city's collective heartbeat.

➤ **The Spark of Mischief in a Glance**. There's a certain spark of mischief to be found in a playful glance. It's the twinkle in your eye as you share a joke at a Chelsea art opening or the impish look during a whimsical moment at a rooftop party. This look speaks of fun, of a shared sense of humor, and a willingness to not take life too seriously, a vital part of the Manhattan spirit.

➤ **The Intrigue of the Inquisitive Eye**. Cultivate the intrigue of the inquisitive eye. It's a look of curiosity, of wanting to know more. Whether you're engaging with a new acquaintance at a Central Park picnic or listening to a street musician in the Village, the inquisitive gaze shows your engagement and interest, inviting others to open up and share their world with you.

➤ **The Strength of Steadfast Gaze**. In moments of decision or conflict, the steadfast gaze is your ally. It's the unwavering eye contact that communicates your resolve and determination, whether it's negotiating a deal in the Financial District or standing your ground in a heated debate. This look is about asserting yourself without saying a word, a silent testament to your inner strength.

➤ **The Dance of the Coy Glance**. Finally, there's the coy glance, a cornerstone in the language of flirtation. It's a quick, shy look away after making eye contact, a subtle game of visual cat and mouse. This glance is all about suggestion, a hint of modest interest.

In The Language of the Look, your eyes become a powerful tool of expression, a way to navigate the myriad relationships and interactions that Manhattan throws your way. It's about understanding that in this city of endless stories, sometimes the most compelling tales are those told not with words, but with glances—a language as complex and nuanced as the city itself. So, darling, as you step into the whirlwind of Manhattan life, let your eyes do the talking, and watch as the world unfolds before you.

Your Triumphs: Speaking with the Eyes Activities

Inspirational Quote

START BY DOING WHAT'S NECESSARY; THEN DO WHAT'S POSSIBLE, AND SUDDENLY YOU ARE DOING THE IMPOSSIBLE. — Francis of Assisi

Your Goals: Intentions and Thoughts

The Intensity of Eye Contact

In the swirling soirees and intimate encounters of Manhattan, where every glance can be a prologue to a new story, The Intensity of Eye Contact is about mastering a gaze that can hold a room or capture a heart. It's the art of locking eyes in a way that's as electrifying as the city's skyline, a connection that's both profound and powerful.

➢ **The Unspoken Depth of the Direct Gaze**. The direct gaze is a silent conversation, an unspoken depth that words often fail to reach. In the candlelit corners of Manhattan's jazz clubs or the bustling, trendy bars of the Lower East Side, a direct, unwavering look speaks of confidence and intrigue. It's a gaze that says, "I see you," a connection that bridges the space between strangers.

➢ **The Magnetism of Measured Eye Contact**. There's a magnetism in measured eye contact, a balancing act between intensity and approachability. It's about maintaining eye contact just long enough to convey interest and sincerity, without overwhelming the other person. In the dance of Manhattan's social interactions, this measured gaze is a step of elegance and finesse.

➢ **The Power Play in Professional Settings**. In the high-stakes boardrooms and negotiation tables, the intensity of eye contact becomes a power play. It's about holding your gaze with a sense of purpose and assurance, asserting your presence in a room where every gesture is a move in the game of ambition and success.

➢ **The Intimacy in the Lingering Look**. There's an undeniable intimacy in a lingering look. In the quiet moments shared on a Central Park bench or across a table in a quaint West Village bistro, a lingering look can communicate more than the most eloquent love letter. It's a gaze that caresses, that holds within it the promise of deeper connections and unspoken understandings.

➤ **The Dance of the Flirting Eyes**. And then there's the dance of flirting eyes—a glance, a look away, and then back again. It's playful, provocative, and quintessentially Manhattan. The eye dance is an artful tease, a way of saying, "I'm interested" without saying anything at all, a delicate game played under the city's glowing lights.

➤ **The Revelation in a Revealing Glance**. In the revealing glance, there's a moment of vulnerability, a brief lowering of the walls we all navigate through life. This look can happen anywhere—in the midst of a laughter-filled party in Tribeca or a chance encounter in a busy Midtown cafe. It's a glance that subtly reveals a hint of your true self, a glimpse into the depths that lie beneath the surface.

➤ **The Challenge in the Steady Stare**. The steady, unblinking stare is often a challenge, a silent dare that speaks of confidence and a bit of audacity. Used judiciously, it's a powerful tool in debates or discussions, a way of non-verbally asserting your stance. In the competitive environment of Manhattan, this gaze can be a testament to your strength and resolve.

➤ **The Spark of Curiosity in the Inquisitive Glance**. Lastly, the inquisitive glance is all about sparking curiosity. It's an open, inviting look that expresses genuine interest and a desire to learn more. This gaze is perfect for engaging with new ideas and perspectives, a way of inviting others to share their stories and experiences, creating a tapestry of shared narratives.

In The Intensity of Eye Contact, your eyes become a tool of enchantment, a way to weave your presence into someone's memory. It's about understanding that in a city of endless narratives, the stories told through the eyes are the most captivating. So, as you navigate the vibrant canvas of Manhattan, let your eyes speak with intensity and grace, crafting connections that are as deep and lasting as the city itself.

Your Triumphs: Silent Communications Activities

Inspirational Quote

TO FIND YOURSELF, THINK FOR YOURSELF. — Socrates

Your Goals: Intentions and Thoughts

The Subtlety in the Soft Glance

In the bustling mosaic of Manhattan, where the bold and the brash often take center stage, The Subtlety in the Soft Glance is an art form in its own right. It's the gentle undercurrent in the river of glances exchanged across the city, a whisper among shouts. In a landscape where eye contact can be as sharp as the city's skyline, the soft glance is a tender melody, a subtle note of intrigue and allure.

➢ **The Allure of the Understated**. In the soft glance lies the allure of the understated. It's a fleeting look, a quick lowering of the lashes, then a gaze that returns just as swiftly. In the crowded bars of the East Village or the teeming streets of Times Square, this soft glance is a breath of subtlety, a hint of mystery amidst the overt.

➢ **The Invitation of the Coy Look**. The coy look is the soft glances' playful cousin. It's the brief meeting of eyes across a room, then a shy look away, only to glance back again. This dance of the eyes is flirtatious yet demure, an invitation wrapped in innocence, a delicate balance that entices and enchants.

➢ **The Gentle Power of Quiet Observation**. The soft glance can also be a tool of quiet observation. In the hushed galleries of the Met or the serene spaces of the New York Public Library, it's a way of taking in the surroundings—and the people—with a gentle curiosity, a way of engaging without intruding, observing without overpowering.

➢ **The Intimacy of the Shared Glimpse**. Sometimes, the soft glance is about sharing a moment. A shared glimpse at a piece of art, a mutual smirk at an inside joke, a simultaneous eye-roll in a meeting—these shared, soft glances create a moment of connection, a silent acknowledgment of a shared experience.

➤ **The Mystery in Momentary Meetings**. There's a profound mystery in those momentary meetings of the eyes. In the busy cafes of Greenwich Village or the bustling streets of the Financial District, a brief, soft glance can be a window to a hidden world, an invitation to ponder the stories behind the eyes. It's a fleeting connection that leaves a lingering question, an enigma wrapped in a simple gaze.

➤ **The Whisper of Shared Secrets**. The soft glance can be like a whisper of shared secrets in a room full of noise. At a glamorous Upper West Side party or a chic gallery opening in Chelsea, exchanging soft glances can create a private world amidst the public space, a silent conversation that speaks of a mutual understanding or a shared amusement.

➤ **The Elegance of Restraint**. In the art of the soft glance, there is an elegance in restraint. It's about expressing interest without overstepping, showing you're intrigued but not invasive. This careful balancing act is a hallmark of true sophistication, a testament to the poise and grace that Manhattanites aspire to.

➤ **The Language of the Linger**. Finally, there's the language of the linger in the soft glance. It's a look that lasts just a fraction longer than necessary, a subtle indication of interest, an unspoken suggestion that there's more to be explored, more to the story than meets the eye.

In The Subtlety in the Soft Glance, it's about understanding that sometimes, the most powerful connections are made in the quietest of moments, with the gentlest of looks. In a city where everyone is vying to be heard, the soft glance is your secret weapon—a way to communicate in whispers, in a world that often only understands shouts. So, darling, as you traverse the vibrant canvas of Manhattan, remember that a soft glance can be just as compelling as the boldest statement.

Your Triumphs: Subtlety and Soft Glances Activities

Inspirational Quote

YOUR TIME IS LIMITED, SO DON'T WASTE IT LIVING SOMEONE ELSE'S LIFE.
— Steve Jobs

Your Goals: Intentions and Thoughts

Mirroring the City's Soul

In the ever-pulsating heart of Manhattan, where every street corner sings a different melody and every skyline tells a different tale, Mirroring the City's Soul is about capturing the essence of this vibrant metropolis in the depths of your gaze. It's a dance of the eyes that reflects the myriad faces of the city, from its dazzling highs to its shadowed lows.

➢ **The Sparkle of Skyline in Your Eyes**. Let your eyes sparkle with the reflection of Manhattan's skyline. Whether you're gazing across the East River at dusk or admiring the neon lights of Times Square, let your eyes hold the city's brilliance, its ambition, its ceaseless energy. Your gaze should be a tapestry of the city's vibrancy, a mirror to its luminous dreams.

➢ **The Depth of the Streets in Your Stare**. There's a depth to be found in a gaze that has witnessed the city's streets—the bustling avenues, the quiet alleys, the hidden corners. Your eyes should tell stories of the diversity and complexity of Manhattan, of the myriad lives and stories that intertwine in this urban jungle.

➢ **The Resilience in the Unwavering Look**. In your unwavering look, let there be a hint of Manhattan's resilience. The city that never sleeps, that rises from trials and tribulations, should be reflected in your steady gaze. It's a look that speaks of perseverance, of an unbreakable spirit, much like the city itself.

➢ **The Melancholy of the Metropolis in a Glance**. And then there's the melancholy, the softer, more introspective side of the city, mirrored in a thoughtful, distant glance. It's the reflective gaze of someone who has seen the city in its quieter moments, who understands the solitude that can exist amidst the crowd.

EYES THAT MESMERIZE

> **The Glimmer of Aspiration in a Glance**. Capture in your gaze the glimmer of aspiration that defines Manhattan. Let your eyes reflect the ambition and the ceaseless striving of its inhabitants. Whether it's the hopeful gaze of an artist in a Lower East Side studio or the determined stare of a young professional in Midtown, your eyes should hold the dreams and aspirations that fuel the city.

> **The Warmth of the Welcoming Eyes**. In a city known for its pace and sometimes its aloofness, let your gaze offer a warmth of welcome. It's the friendly twinkle in your eyes as you navigate the crowded streets of the Upper West Side or sit in the bustling cafes of Harlem. This warm, welcoming look is an invitation, a signal of openness in a city that can sometimes close in on itself.

> **The Reflection of the City's Pulse in Your Pupils**. In the rapid movement of your gaze, mimic the ever-changing, dynamic rhythm of Manhattan. It's a visual rhythm that captures the pulse of the city—from the serene mornings in Riverside Park to the electric nights in the Meatpacking District.

> **The Whisper of Shared Humanity in a Look**. Finally, let your eyes reflect the shared humanity found in the streets of Manhattan. In a city teeming with life, every glance can be an acknowledgment of a shared existence, a moment of connection in the vast tapestry of urban life.

In Mirroring the City's Soul, your gaze becomes a homage to the city, a reflection of its myriad moods and stories. It's about letting your eyes be a canvas where the city paints its tales—tales of wonder, of struggle, of beauty, and of resilience. So, darling, as you lock eyes with fellow New Yorkers or with those who dream of the city from afar, let your gaze be as deep and varied as Manhattan itself—a testament to the city that never fails to captivate and inspire.

Your Triumphs: Mirroring the City's Soul Activities

Your Triumphs: Mirroring the City's Soul Activities

Inspirational Quote

IT IS NEVER TOO LATE TO BE WHAT YOU MIGHT HAVE BEEN. — George Eliot

Your Goals: Intentions and Thoughts

Your Goals: Intentions and Thoughts

5

The Sound of Silence: Knowing When to Pause and Power Up the Intrigue

Manhattan, a city of whispers and roars, where every heartbeat seems to sync with the rhythm of subway trains and honking cabs. Yet, among these endless sounds, the most potent weapon of a Manhattanite isn't always in speaking, but in knowing when to stay silent—allowing intrigue to fill the spaces between.

Now imagine: You're sipping a cocktail at The Carlyle, surrounded by the city's crème de la crème. The conversation around you is a symphony of stories, laughter, and dreams. But instead of jumping in, you choose a strategic pause, letting the room hang on that delicious note of anticipation. That, darling, is the Manhattan Pause—a display of restraint, wisdom, and a tantalizing hint of the unknown.

In this electrifying chapter of The Manhattan Diaries, we'll dive deep into the art of silence. From the deliberate pause in a heated debate to the lingering silence shared with a stranger across a crowded bar, we'll explore the power of saying everything by saying nothing at all.

But this isn't just about holding back—no. It's about understanding the city's rhythm, recognizing the moments when less truly is more. It's about reading the room, gauging the air, and striking when the moment is perfectly ripe. It's about harnessing the strength of the city's shadows and its glowing lights, and understanding the dance between the two.

Join me, as we traverse the city's bustling avenues and quiet corners, mastering the art of the pause that not only halts you but the world around you. Because, sweetheart, in Manhattan, every silence is an opportunity, a canvas waiting for your next move. Brace yourself, for the city is listening, waiting for your encore. Welcome to The Manhattan Diaries—where your silence can be as captivating as the city's most enchanting sonnet.

The Intrigue of the Intentional Pause

In the high-stakes chess game of Manhattan's social circles, where every word can be a move and every silence a strategy, The Intrigue of the Intentional Pause is your secret weapon. It's about mastering the art of the deliberate silence, the pause that speaks louder than words. This isn't just about stopping to take a breath; it's about crafting a moment of anticipation, a space charged with possibility and promise.

➤ **The Dramatic Pause in Conversation**. Imagine you're in the midst of a tantalizing story at a cocktail party overlooking Central Park. You reach the climax, and then—you pause. It's a dramatic halt, a moment that hangs in the air like a note in a jazz solo. Your audience leans in, captivated. This pause is a conductor's baton, controlling the rhythm of the conversation, heightening the drama, the tension, the excitement.

➤ **The Reflective Silence**. Then there's the reflective silence, a thoughtful lull in a deeper, more introspective discussion. Perhaps you're at a gallery in Chelsea, discussing the art. A question is posed, and instead of diving in with an immediate response, you pause. This silence isn't empty; it's laden with thought, suggesting a depth and a seriousness that invites others to ponder along with you.

➤ **The Flirtatious Hesitation**. The flirtatious hesitation is an art form on its own. It's the brief pause before a smile, the moment of eye contact just a second too long. In the dimly lit bars of the Lower East Side or the bustling cafes of the West Village, these pauses are the language of flirtation, a non-verbal dance that teases and entices.

➤ **The Power Pause in Negotiation**. In the boardrooms and business lunches, the power pause is a tool of influence. When negotiating, a pause before you answer, before you counter an offer, can be disarming. It communicates confidence, control, and an unspoken assertion that you're considering your options, weighing your power.

> **The Suspense-Building Halt**. Utilize the suspense-building halt to captivate your audience. Picture yourself recounting an enthralling experience at an Upper East Side dinner party. Just as you approach the climax of your tale, you pause. This intentional break builds suspense, drawing your listeners closer into your narrative web, hanging on your every unsaid word, eager for the conclusion.

> **The Pause of Poise in Debate**. In the lively debates that sparkle across Manhattan's intellectual gatherings, use the pause of poise. When presented with a challenging viewpoint, a moment of silence before your response demonstrates composure and contemplation. It's a signal that you're considering the argument thoughtfully, not just reacting, showcasing your elegance under pressure.

> **The Intimacy of the Lingering Pause**. In intimate setting, the lingering pause can be profoundly effective. Imagine a quiet moment in a cozy West Village cafe, where a lingering silence in your conversation opens a space for unspoken emotions and deepening connections. It's a tacit invitation for the other person to share more, to delve deeper into the conversation.

> **The Strategic Pause for Emphasis**. When delivering an important message or presenting an idea, a well-paced pause can underline a key point, allowing it to resonate powerfully with your audience.

In The Intrigue of the Intentional Pause, it's about using silence to your advantage, creating moments that are as charged and as potent as any spoken word. It's a skill that, when mastered, gives you an edge in the city's never-ending ballet of social and professional interactions. So, darling, as you navigate the whirlwind of Manhattan, remember: sometimes the most powerful thing you can say is nothing at all.

Your Triumphs: Intentional Pauses Activities

Inspirational Quote

LIFE IS LIKE RIDING A BICYCLE. TO KEEP YOUR BALANCE, YOU MUST KEEP MOVING. — Albert Einstein

Your Goals: Intentions and Thoughts

The Elegance of Listening

In the whirlwind of Manhattan's endless chatter, where words often race by like taxis down Fifth Avenue, The Elegance of Listening emerges as a rare and refined art. It's about cultivating a presence that invites confidences and secrets, turning a simple conversation into an intimate tango of shared experiences and understanding.

- ➤ **The Allure of Attentive Silence.** There's an undeniable allure in being the one who listens, truly listens. In the cacophony of a Manhattan cocktail party or the buzz of a trendy SoHo cafe, being the person who offers the gift of attentive silence is like being a beacon of calm in a sea of noise. It's about lending your ears, offering your undivided attention, and in doing so, making the speaker feel like the only person in the room.

- ➤ **The Charm of the Reflective Response.** The elegance of listening is also in the reflective response. It's not about merely waiting for your turn to speak, but absorbing, processing, and then responding in a way that shows you've truly heard. This can transform a casual chat on a rooftop lounge into a meaningful exchange, a conversation that lingers long after the city lights fade.

- ➤ **The Magnetism of Empathetic Engagement.** Engaging empathically with the speaker's emotions is a magnetic quality. Whether it's sharing a moment of joy, understanding a disappointment, or empathizing with a struggle, the ability to tune into and reflect back these emotions is a hallmark of a great listener. It's a skill that turns acquaintances into confidants, conversations into connections.

- ➤ **The Grace of Encouraging More.** Master the grace of encouraging more from the speaker. It's about gently nudging the narrative along with thoughtful questions or prompts, showing genuine interest in peeling back the layers of the story. In the diverse tapestry of Manhattan, where everyone has a story to tell, being the person who encourages those stories to unfold is a truly elegant role.

> **The Resonance of Non-verbal Acknowledgment.** Non-verbal cues play a vital role. A nod, a smile, a slight tilt of the head—these subtle gestures can resonate deeply, signaling that you're fully engaged. In the bustling brunch spots of the Upper West Side or the intimate jazz clubs of Greenwich Village, these silent affirmations make your conversational partner feel truly seen and heard.

> **The Wisdom in Knowing When to Speak.** The elegance of listening also lies in knowing when to interject, when to add your thoughts, and when to simply stay quiet. It's a delicate balance, a dance of timing and tact. Whether you're at an exclusive gallery opening or a casual gathering in Brooklyn, understanding when your words will enhance the conversation and when your silence will empower the speaker is key.

> **The Gift of Giving Undivided Attention.** In a city where distractions abound, giving someone your undivided attention is a priceless gift. It means putting away the phone, stepping away from the buzz of constant connectivity, and focusing solely on the person in front of you. In the competitive environment, this level of attention can set you apart, marking you as a listener of rare quality.

In The Elegance of Listening, the act of lending an ear becomes as significant as lending a voice. It's about recognizing that sometimes, the most profound way to engage in the narrative of the city is to simply listen, to absorb the tales, the dreams, the hopes, and the fears that pulse through its streets. So, darling, as you grace the myriad gatherings of Manhattan, remember that the art of listening can be your most captivating accessory—one that adorns not only you but those who have the joy of your company.

Your Triumphs: The Art of Listening Activities

Inspirational Quote

JUST DON'T GIVE UP TRYING TO DO WHAT YOU REALLY WANT TO DO. WHERE THERE IS LOVE AND INSPIRATION, I DON'T THINK YOU CAN GO WRONG. — Ella Fitzgerald

Your Goals: Intentions and Thoughts

The Drama of the Unsaid

In the captivating canvas of Manhattan, where every word carries the weight of a Broadway show, The Drama of the Unsaid stands out as a compelling act in the city's endless play. It's about the power of what's left unsaid, the tantalizing tales that linger in the silence, a potent narrative told in the spaces between words.

> ➤ **The Allure of Unspoken Mystery**. There's an irresistible allure in the unspoken mystery. In the softly lit corners of exclusive Upper East Side lounges or amidst the clinking glasses of downtown speakeasies, what you don't say often holds more intrigue than what you do. It's the unsaid that invites speculation, that draws people in, craving to know more.

> ➤ **The Silent Dance of Seduction**. In the realm of romance, the unsaid is a silent dance of seduction. It's the lingering look that says everything and nothing, the subtle smile that hints but doesn't reveal. In Manhattan's dating scene, where mystery is as alluring as the promise of romance, the unsaid becomes a language of its own.

> ➤ **The Weight of Wordless Implications**. In the boardrooms and power lunches of Wall Street, the unsaid can be heavy with implications. A pause in a negotiation, a withheld comment in a meeting—these silences can be strategic, calculated moves that speak louder than the most eloquent rhetoric.

> ➤ **The Unvoiced Emotional Undercurrent**. Sometimes, the most profound connections are forged in what's not said. In the intimate settings of a friend's apartment or a quiet bench in Battery Park, the comfort of sitting together in silence often says more about your bond than any conversation could. It's the unsaid that weaves an emotional undercurrent, a shared understanding beyond words.

➢ **The Power of Suggestion in Social Settings**. In the social whirl of Manhattan, suggestion is your silent ally. It's the art of hinting at a possibility, a future plan, or a shared secret without giving it all away. Whether at a rooftop party in Tribeca or a Broadway after-party, these hints and suggestions create a web of intrigue and anticipation, making your presence enigmatic and memorable.

➢ **The Silent Strength of Restraint**. There's a silent strength in restraint, in choosing not to respond or engage in a moment of tension or conflict. In high-energy environments, from tense corporate meetings to passionate debates in a Midtown bar, knowing when to hold back, to let the silence speak, is a show of control and composure, a subtle demonstration of power and self-assuredness.

➢ **The Unvoiced Connection in Shared Glances**. Sometimes, a shared glance can communicate more than a flurry of words. It's the unspoken acknowledgment between two people who find themselves in mutual understanding or shared amusement—a silent nod to a burgeoning friendship or alliance.

➢ **The Artful Omission in Storytelling**. Lastly, there's an art to omission in storytelling. Whether recounting an anecdote at a SoHo art opening or sharing experiences over coffee in Greenwich Village, it's the details you leave out that often spark the imagination, enticing your audience to fill in the blanks, drawing them deeper into your narrative.

In The Drama of the Unsaid, the silence is as eloquent as the speech, each pause a stage for the audience's imagination to perform. It's about understanding that in the bustling script of Manhattan, the most compelling stories often lie in what's not said, in the hidden depths and shadows of the unspoken. So, darling, as you navigate the city's grand narrative, remember: the drama of the unsaid can be your most captivating performance.

Your Triumphs: Silent Interludes Activities

Inspirational Quote

LIMIT YOUR 'ALWAYS' AND YOUR 'NEVERS.' — Amy Poehler

Your Goals: Intentions and Thoughts

The Mastery of Timing in Silence

In the pulsating rhythm of Manhattan, where timing is as crucial as the latest fashion trend, The Mastery of Timing in Silence is akin to hitting the perfect note in a symphony. It's about understanding that sometimes the most impactful statement is a well-placed moment of silence, a pause that speaks louder than words ever could.

➤ **The Art of Pausing Before the Punchline**. Imagine you're at a glittering event in a luxurious Midtown penthouse, sharing a story that has the room's undivided attention. The art lies in pausing just before the punchline, creating a delicious tension that makes the finale all the more impactful. It's a theatrical technique, a dramatic pause that amplifies the laughter and response from your captivated audience.

➤ **The Reflective Hush in Conversations**. In deeper, more meaningful conversations, perhaps in the quieter corners of a bustling Manhattan cafe or a serene walk along the High Line, the reflective hush is vital. It's about giving space after a significant point or emotional revelation, allowing the words to resonate, to settle in the listener's heart. This silence is a sign of respect and empathy, an acknowledgment of the weight of words shared.

➤ **The Pause of Anticipation in Flirtation**. On the romantic front, a pause can be tantalizingly effective. Amidst the flirtatious banter of a chic downtown bar, a pause can be laden with anticipation, a silent invitation for the other person to lean in, both figuratively and literally. It's a non-verbal tease, a way of heightening the intrigue and attraction without a single word.

➤ **The Silent Acknowledgement of Shared Moments**. Sometimes, in the shared silence, lies the deepest connection. It might be a quiet moment of mutual understanding with a close friend in the midst of the Central Park's hustle, or a silent, shared laugh over an inside joke. These silences are the unspoken threads that strengthen the bonds of friendship and love.

➤ **The Calculated Lull in Group Dynamics**. Within the buzzing social scenes of Manhattan, from rooftop parties to bustling brunches, mastering the calculated lull can shift the group dynamics. It's about strategically inserting a moment of silence in a group conversation, a pause that can redirect the flow of dialogue, subtly shifting the focus or allowing someone else to take the floor—it demonstrates your social acumen and respect for the conversation.

➤ **The Introspective Pause in Personal Stories**. When sharing personal stories, particularly in more intimate settings like a cozy wine bar in the Village, the introspective pause adds layers to your narrative. It's a moment of reflection, suggesting that your story is not just a rehearsed tale but a piece of your lived experience.

➤ **The Dramatic Pause for Effect**. Lastly, there's the dramatic pause for effect, a tool used by the best storytellers and public speakers. Whether you're captivating an audience at a gallery opening in Chelsea or making a toast at a wedding in a grand Manhattan ballroom, a well-timed dramatic pause can enhance the impact of your words, creating suspense and heightening the audience's emotional response.

In The Mastery of Timing in Silence, it's about harnessing the power of the unsaid, of using silence not as an absence of communication, but as a profound form of it. In a city that thrives on noise and constant chatter, the ability to use silence strategically can make you stand out, lending a depth and intrigue to your persona. So, as you navigate the vibrant tapestry of Manhattan, remember that sometimes the most compelling thing you can do is to say nothing at all.

Your Triumphs: The Art of Timed Silence Activities

Inspirational Quote

NOTHING IS IMPOSSIBLE. THE WORD ITSELF SAYS 'I'M POSSIBLE!' — Audrey Hepburn

Your Goals: Intentions and Thoughts

Your Goals: Intentions and Thoughts

6

Glamour On the Go:
New York Nights and Taxi Cab Confessions

Manhattan, a city that twinkles under a starlit canopy of skyscrapers and dreams. Here, time doesn't merely tick; it dazzles, especially as twilight descends, and the city's glamorati emerge, painting the town in hues of allure and aspiration. It isn't just about reaching your destination in this concrete wonderland; it's about the journey, the shimmer, and the stories shared in the backseat of a yellow cab.

Now imagine: You're stepping out of a Broadway show, sequins catching the neon lights, as you hail a cab on Seventh Avenue. Heads turn, not just because of the designer shoes you wear, but the tantalizing tales you tell. That, my darling, is the essence of Taxi Cab Glamour, an arena where secrets spill, dreams dance, and the night feels forever young.

In this intoxicating chapter of The Manhattan Diaries, we'll journey through the city's veins in its iconic yellow chariots, uncovering tales of love, loss, and everything in-between. From whispered confessions after a SoHo soiree to the impassioned dreams shared en route to an Upper East Side penthouse, you'll learn the art of captivating cab confessions.

But this isn't merely about whispered words or stolen glances—no. It's about the rhythm of the city night, the mosaic of stories it shelters, and the intoxicating allure of fleeting moments. It's about recognizing that every cab ride can be an odyssey, an adventure, a serendipitous encounter.

Join me, as we navigate Manhattan's illuminated streets, embracing every twist, turn, and tantalizing tale. Because, sweetheart, in Manhattan, every cab ride is a scene waiting to be written, a drama longing to unfold. So, slide into that backseat, share a secret or two, and let the city be your ever-eager audience. Welcome to The Manhattan Diaries—where your cab confessions can be as mesmerizing as the city's most legendary tales.

The Intimacy of the Confined Space

In the pulsating heart of Manhattan, where the city's energy is as boundless as its skyline, The Intimacy of the Confined Space of a taxi cab becomes an unexpected sanctuary. Here, amidst the blur of neon and the symphony of urban chaos, the backseat of a yellow cab transforms into a private state, a place where secrets are safe and confessions are sacred.

- ➢ **The Whispered Confidences in Close Quarters**. Picture yourself gliding through the streets of Manhattan, the city lights casting shadows inside the cab. In this small, intimate space, conversations naturally turn more personal, more profound. It's as if the closeness of the cab's interior invites whispered confidences, encourages the sharing of stories that might never be told in the openness of a crowded room.

- ➢ **The Magic of Manhattan's Moving Microcosm**. The taxi cab is a microcosm of Manhattan itself—vibrant, ever-moving, full of stories. As the cityscape rushes by your window, there's a sense of being in a world apart, a transient bubble where time and space condense. In this moving microcosm, the barriers come down, and the conversation delves into depths that the sprawling city outside might not allow.

- ➢ **The Solace in the City's Heartbeat**. Amidst the constant heartbeat of the city, the backseat of a cab offers a rare solace. Here, you can lean back, let the city's pulse become a backdrop, and truly connect with your fellow passenger. Whether it's a ride with a long-time friend or a chance encounter with a stranger, the cab's confined space fosters an environment where words flow more freely, where the heart speaks as loudly as the mind.

➤ **The Theatricality of the Enclosed Stage**. And then there's the theatricality of this enclosed stage. Each ride becomes a scene in the larger play of your Manhattan life. The conversations here are heightened, more dramatic, charged with the energy of the city itself. It's a space where mundane moments can turn into memorable scenes, where ordinary nights can transform into tales worth retelling.

➤ **The Comfort of Anonymity in Motion**. In the transient anonymity of a taxi's backseat, there's a unique comfort that encourages openness. The city flies by, a faceless blur, as you find yourself sharing thoughts and dreams with a near-stranger or a newfound acquaintance. This anonymity in motion offers a liberating sense of detachment, a fleeting escape from the identities and roles played out in the static spaces of daily life.

➤ **The Fusion of Lives in Shared Journeys**. Every shared cab ride through Manhattan is a fusion of lives, an unexpected intertwining of narratives. These are the rides where destinies briefly align—the artist heading to a gallery opening in Chelsea, the banker en route to a late-night deal downtown. In the confines of the cab, their stories overlap, offering glimpses into worlds that may have never intersected otherwise.

In The Intimacy of the Confined Space, the backseat of a Manhattan taxi cab becomes more than just a means of transportation; it becomes a haven of human connection. It's where the city's relentless energy is distilled into quiet, meaningful exchanges, where the stories of a million lives intersect in the most personal of ways. So, darling, next time you find yourself in the back of a cab, cruising down the avenues and alleys of the city, open up to the intimacy of the moment—for in these close quarters, the true spirit of Manhattan often reveals itself.

Your Triumphs: Unexpected Sanctuaries Activities

Inspirational Quote

YOU ARE NEVER TOO OLD TO SET ANOTHER GOAL OR TO DREAM A NEW DREAM. — C. S. Lewis

Your Goals: Intentions and Thoughts

The Romance of the Nighttime Journey

In the enchanting twilight hours of Manhattan, when the city transforms into a glittering stage of possibilities, The Romance of the Nighttime Journey in a taxi cab becomes a quintessential New York experience. It's a time when the ordinary becomes extraordinary, and every red light is a chance to fall in love—with the city, with the night, with a stranger's story.

- ➤ **The Magic of the City Lights**. Picture this: you're gliding through the streets, the city lights flickering like diamonds against the sky. There's something about New York at night—that turns a simple cab ride into a journey through a modern-day fairytale. Each turn brings a new vista, a new scene in this urban romance.

- ➤ **The Intimacy of Shared Destinations**. In the shared destination of a nighttime cab ride, there's an unexpected intimacy. You're both heading somewhere—maybe to a party in a penthouse, a rendezvous in a hidden jazz club, or just home after a long day. In these moments, the city outside the windows feels both vast and intimate, and the shared journey becomes a thread in the tapestry of the night.

- ➤ **The Serendipity of Chance Encounters**. The nighttime cab ride is ripe with the serendipity of chance encounters. It's a rolling oasis where paths cross and fates intertwine. You might share a ride with a future best friend, a lover, or a kindred spirit. Under the soft glow of the cab's interior light, strangers become confidants, sharing laughs, secrets, or even just comfortable silence.

- ➤ **The Whisper of Unspoken Promises**. There are the unspoken promises that hang in the air of a nighttime taxi—promises of adventure, of stories waiting to be written. Whether it's the shared glance with a fellow passenger or a quiet moment of reflection as you pass by the twinkling lights of the Empire State Building, each ride is a promise of the endless potential that the night holds.

> **The Narrative of the City at Night.** Every nighttime cab ride in Manhattan is like a chapter in the city's ongoing narrative. As you traverse through the neon-lit lanes of Times Square or the quiet, tree-lined streets of the West Village, each block tells its own story. The city at night reveals a different character, one that's more intimate and raw. Your journey becomes a part of this larger narrative, a fleeting yet significant moment in the grand tapestry of New York after dark.

> **The Introspection of the Solo Ride.** For those solo rides back home or to the next destination, there's a unique introspection that the night invites. The city's skyline passing by your window becomes a backdrop for reflection, a time to think about the day past or dream about the days to come. It's a personal moment with the city, where the solitude of the cab ride offers a rare opportunity for self-connection amidst the ceaseless beat of urban life.

> **The Connection in Shared Silence.** Often, the most romantic aspect of a nighttime cab ride is the shared silence. With someone beside you, the silent journey through the city streets can be an unspoken communion, a shared appreciation of the city's beauty and its quiet moments. This silence is comfortable and intimate, and speaks of a deep connection that goes beyond words.

In The Romance of the Nighttime Journey, the backseat of a cab becomes a liminal space where the magic of Manhattan nights is not just witnessed but lived. It's a place where the journey matters as much as the destination, where every ride is an opportunity to fall a little more in love with the city's nocturnal enchantment. So, darling, as you journey through the streets of Manhattan under the starlit sky, let the romance of the ride whisk you away, if only for a moment, into the city's loving embrace.

Your Triumphs: City Rhythmic Pace Activities

Inspirational Quote

TRY TO BE A RAINBOW IN SOMEONE ELSE'S CLOUD. — Maya Angelou

Your Goals: Intentions and Thoughts

The Catharsis of the Cab Confession

In the pulsing heart of Manhattan, where secrets are as plentiful as the stars above the city skyline, The Catharsis of the Cab Confession emerges as a quintessential New York experience. It's in the backseat of a cruising taxi, amidst the blur of neon lights and towering skyscrapers, where the most guarded hearts often find the freedom to unburden, where the soul finds its unexpected confessional.

➢ **The Liberation of Anonymity**. There's something liberating about confiding in a stranger, especially when encased in the transient intimacy of a taxi. Whether it's to the driver, a mere silhouette under the dim dashboard lights, or to a fellow passenger, the anonymity provides a safe haven. Here, you can divulge your deepest fears, your wildest dreams, or your most absurd anecdotes without the fear of judgment. The city keeps moving, and so do your secrets, dispersed into the night.

➢ **The Unlikely Bond of Shared Stories**. Picture this: You're sharing a cab across the island, from the glittering lights of Midtown to the quiet, shadowed streets of the East Village. What starts as small talk evolves into a heart-to-heart, a sharing of stories that creates an unlikely bond. In the unique closeness of the cab, people find common ground, a mutual understanding that transcends their disparate lives outside.

➢ **The Relief of Unspoken Burdens**. In the confessional of the cab, there's a palpable relief that comes from voicing thoughts and feelings that have been unspoken far too long. It could be a confession of love, a revelation of personal truth, or a simple admission of a day gone wrong. Each confession, set against the backdrop of the city's ceaseless rhythm, feels like a small but significant unburdening of the soul.

➢ **The Serendipity of Unexpected Advice.** And then there are those moments of unexpected advice, the wisdom offered by a driver who's seen it all or a passenger who just happens to say the right thing at the right time. In these serendipitous exchanges, the cab becomes a rolling oracle, dispensing insights and perspectives that resonate with surprising depth.

➢ **The Unraveling of the Night's Narrative.** As the city transitions from dusk to dawn, the taxi cab becomes a stage where the night's narrative unravels. Each passenger brings their own storyline—a triumph at a gallery opening, a setback in a Broadway audition, a romantic encounter turned bittersweet. In the cab's confined space, these narratives find a voice, a cathartic release that allows for closure and, sometimes, a new beginning.

➢ **The Healing Power of a Listening Ear.** There's a profound healing power in simply being heard, and the taxi cab often provides this therapeutic space. Whether it's the empathetic ear of a driver who's mastered the art of listening or the understanding nod of a fellow passenger, these moments of being heard can be profoundly healing. In a city where everyone is perpetually busy, these instances of genuine attention can transform a routine cab ride into a moment of true connection.

In The Catharsis of the Cab Confession, the act of revealing one's inner world amidst the anonymity of the city's veins becomes a moment of unexpected release. It's a testament to the power of human connection, to the unexpected intimacy that can arise in the most unlikely of places. So, as you glide through the streets of Manhattan remember that sometimes, a cab ride can be more than just a journey from point A to point B; it can be a journey within, a moment to confess, to connect, to cathartically embrace the beautiful complexity of human experience.

Your Triumphs: Taxi Confessionals Activities

_____

_____

_____

_____

_____

_____

_____

_____

_____

_____

_____

_____

_____

_____

_____

_____

_____

_____

_____

_____

_____

_____

_____

_____

_____

Inspirational Quote

INSPIRATION EXISTS, BUT IT MUST FIND YOU WORKING. — Pablo Picasso

Your Goals: Intentions and Thoughts

The Serendipity of Shared Rides

In the ever-twisting, ever-turning narrative of Manhattan, The Serendipity of Shared Rides plays out like an enchanting subplot in the city's grand story. It's in these shared taxi rides, a modern-day carriage of happenstance, where the city's diverse tapestry of souls come together, creating moments of unexpected connection and delightful coincidence.

➢ **The Dance of Chance Encounters**. Imagine stepping into a cab on a rainy evening in SoHo, sharing the ride with someone who, under any other circumstance, might have remained a stranger. Yet, in the serendipity of shared rides, these strangers become co-stars in a fleeting vignette of city life. A conversation strikes up, a shared laugh over the day's chaos, a mutual admiration for a hidden jazz club. In these moments, the city shrinks, and the vast web of Manhattan becomes intimately personal.

➢ **The Mosaic of Manhattan's Characters**. Each shared ride is a kaleidoscope of the city's characters. You might find yourself alongside an aspiring Broadway actor, a Wall Street banker, or an artist with paint still fresh on their hands. These rides become a microcosm of the city itself, a place where stories and lives intersect in a colorful mosaic of humanity.

➢ **The Unexpected Friendships**. Sometimes, these shared rides blossom into unexpected friendships. A conversation that starts in the backseat of a cab heading uptown can lead to an exchange of numbers, a coffee meetup, or even a lasting bond. In the whirlwind of city life, where making connections can be as daunting as navigating the subway map, shared rides offer a rare opportunity to forge new, serendipitous friendships.

➢ **The Shared Witness of the City's Beauty**. Then there's the shared witness of the city's beauty. As the cab moves through the iconic streets, passengers often find themselves united in their awe of the city's landmarks, its skyline, its spontaneous street performances. In these moments, the ride becomes a collective experience, a shared appreciation for the ever-evolving canvas of New York.

> **The Romance of Unplanned Journeys**. Occasionally, shared taxi rides in Manhattan turn into chapters of a romantic tale. Picture a late-night ride where a chance encounter leads to exchanged glances, tentative conversations, and the spark of something new. In the city that never sleeps, these rides can be the beginning of a whirlwind romance, a serendipitous meeting of hearts amidst the urban hustle.

> **The Wisdom of Collective Experiences**. In the confined space of a cab, passengers often share more than just a physical journey; they share wisdom and insights. It could be a life lesson from a seasoned New Yorker, career advice from a successful entrepreneur, or artistic inspiration from a fellow creative soul. These shared rides become impromptu forums for wisdom, where the city's knowledge and experiences are passed on in the most unlikely of classrooms.

> **The Joy of Shared Discoveries**. Perhaps, a fellow passenger might mention an off-the-beaten-path eatery in Chinatown or a must-see exhibit at a lesser-known museum. These rides can become treasure troves of insider tips and recommendations, helping you discover hidden gems of the city that you might have otherwise missed.

In The Serendipity of Shared Rides, the humble backseat of a taxi cab becomes a stage for the city's unpredictable narrative, a space where paths cross and fates intertwine. It's a reminder that in Manhattan's grand and bustling milieu, magic can be found in the simplest of settings—a shared cab ride under the city lights. So, darling, the next time you slide into a shared ride, be open to the serendipity of the encounter—for in these moments, the city offers its most unexpected gifts.

Your Triumphs: Unexpected Connections Activities

Inspirational Quote

YOU DO NOT FIND THE HAPPY LIFE. YOU MAKE IT. — Camilla Eyring Kimball

Your Goals: Intentions and Thoughts

Your Goals: Intentions and Thoughts

7

Rooftop Reveries:
Rising Above and Holding Court with the Stars

Manhattan, a city where the sky isn't just up above—it's a canvas, dotted with rooftop oases where the city's elite rendezvous under starlit umbrellas. Amid the cacophony of taxi horns and subway rumbles, there lies an elevated serenity, where ambition takes a breath, and desires dance with the constellations. In this city of dizzying heights, it's not just about scaling the corporate ladder or your apartment's elevator—it's about ascending with style, mystique, and a cocktail in hand.

Now imagine: You're stepping out onto a rooftop bar in the Meatpacking District, the golden hue of twilight bathing you. Eyes are drawn not because of the glint of your jewelry, but the aura with which you command the horizon. That, darling, is the Manhattan Rooftop Radiance, a spectacle that speaks of elegance, allure, and a mastery over the metropolitan maze below.

In this mesmerizing chapter of The Manhattan Diaries, we delve into the art of rooftop reveries. From the coy elegance of a penthouse soiree in the Upper East Side to the electrifying vibes of a downtown DJ set, you'll master the craft of holding court with the cosmos, cocktail in hand.

But this isn't just about the breathtaking views or the bubbling champagne—no. It's about capturing the city's pulse from above, about being part of a celestial narrative while rooted in urban magnificence. It's about understanding that while Manhattan hustles below, up here, we compose sonnets, toast to dreams, and dance with the stars.

Join me, as we ascend above the city's frenzy, embracing the tranquility, the panoramas, and the heady conversations that only a Manhattan rooftop can offer. Because, sweetheart, up here, every whispered secret carries the weight of a constellation. Every laugh, every clink of a glass echoes eternity. Welcome to The Manhattan Diaries—where your rooftop rendezvous can be as legendary as the city's most iconic skyscrapers.

The Glamour of Twilight Ascension

In the enchanting transition from day to night, The Glamour of Twilight Ascension captures the essence of ascending to Manhattan's rooftop realms as twilight blankets the city. This moment, rich in anticipation and allure, is where the day's hustle yields to the night's promise, a time when the city's pulse merges with the rhythm of the stars.

➤ **The Transformation of Dusk.** As the sun sets, Manhattan undergoes a metamorphosis. The fading daylight gives way to the city's evening attire, draped in the seductive glow of twilight. This change sets the stage for a night of glamour and mystery.

➤ **Elevated Departure from Daily Life.** Stepping onto a rooftop as twilight descends is a departure from the mundane. It's an elevation not just in height but in spirit. As you ascend, the noise and chaos of the city streets fall away, replaced by a serene anticipation of the night's potential.

➤ **The First Glimpse of the City Lights.** The moment you emerge onto the rooftop, the first glimpse of the city's lights igniting under the twilight sky is breathtaking. It's a scene that captures the heart of Manhattan's magic—the blend of urban energy and celestial calm.

➤ **The Aura of Twilight's First Stars.** In this liminal time, the first stars of the evening begin to twinkle in the deepening blue sky. Their appearance adds a touch of cosmic wonder to the rooftop setting, reminding revelers of the vast universe beyond the city's heights.

➤ **The Silhouette of Skyscrapers.** As the sky darkens, the silhouettes of Manhattan's skyscrapers become striking outlines against the twilight. They stand as monuments to ambition and dreams, framing the rooftop experience with a sense of awe and grandeur.

➢ **The Allure of Rooftop Ambiance**. With the arrival of twilight, the rooftop ambiance is charged with excitement and elegance. The soft lighting, the murmur of conversations, and the clinking of glasses create an atmosphere that is both intimate and vibrant.

➢ **The Sense of Escape and Freedom**. Twilight on a rooftop offers a sense of escape. It's a momentary liberation from the confines of walls and schedules, a breath of freedom where the sky is the limit, both literally and figuratively.

➢ **The Transition from Worker to Reveler**. As daylight fades, so does the identity of the worker, the commuter, the day-to-day city dweller. In its place emerges the reveler, the dreamer, the nighttime persona ready to embrace the mysteries and pleasures of the city after dark.

➢ **The Intimacy of Shared Twilight Moments**. These twilight moments on the rooftop are often shared, whether with old friends or new acquaintances. They are times of connection, where conversations and laughter mingle with the soft city sounds from below, creating bonds forged in the beauty of the evening.

➢ **The Anticipation of Night's Enchantment**. As twilight deepens into night, there's a palpable sense of anticipation for the hours ahead. It's a time when possibilities are endless, when the night promises its own stories and adventures, all beginning from the glamourous heights of Manhattan's rooftops.

The Glamour of Twilight Ascension is not just a transition from day to night; it's a journey into the heart of New York's nocturnal enchantment. It's a celebration of the city's dual nature—its grounded hustle and its soaring aspirations, all witnessed from the elevated vantage point of its glittering rooftops.

Your Triumphs: Twilight Glamour Activities

Inspirational Quote

THE MOST WASTED OF DAYS IS ONE WITHOUT LAUGHTER. — E. E. Cummings

Your Goals: Intentions and Thoughts

Commanding the Horizon

Commanding the Horizon captures the exhilarating experience of dominating the skyline from the unique vantage point of Manhattan's rooftops. It's about the magnetic allure of standing above the cityscape, where the horizon is not just a distant line, but a realm of endless possibilities, a stage for the bold and the beautiful.

> ➤ **The Majesty of the Skyline**. From the rooftop, the city's skyline unfolds in all its grandeur, a tapestry of architectural marvels. Standing amidst this, one feels a part of something larger, a commander of concrete and dreams, surveying a kingdom of steel and glass.

> ➤ **Silhouetted Against the Sky**. As you gaze out over the city, your silhouette becomes one with the horizon. In this moment, you are not just observing the city; you are an integral part of its narrative, a figure etched against the vast canvas of New York.

> ➤ **The Power of Perspective**. From this elevated perspective, the bustling streets below seem a world away. The chaos of traffic, the weave of pedestrians—all appear as orchestrated movements in an urban ballet, offering a sense of control and detachment.

> ➤ **Eyes as Beacons**. On the rooftop, your gaze becomes a beacon, casting across the buildings and streets. There's a sense of ownership in this look, a feeling of reigning over the vast expanse, with each light twinkling back as if in acknowledgment.

> ➤ **The Intimacy of the Vast Sky**. Above you, the vastness of the sky creates an intimate canopy. It's a paradoxical feeling—being exposed to the enormity of the universe, yet finding a personal connection with the cosmos, a dialogue with the stars.

➢ **The Horizon as a Metaphor.** The horizon here is more than a physical boundary; it's a metaphor for ambition and aspiration. It represents the limitless potential of the city and those who dare to dream within it.

➢ **A Moment of Conquest.** Standing on a rooftop, commanding the horizon, is a moment of conquest, not just over the city, but over one's own limitations. It's a testament to the heights one can reach, both literally and figuratively, in the pursuit of greatness.

➢ **The Dance of Light and Shadow.** As day turns to night, the interplay of light and shadow on the rooftops adds to the drama of commanding the horizon. The setting sun casts long shadows, while the emerging city lights begin to sparkle, each contributing to the feeling of dominion over the city's pulse.

➢ **The Whisper of the Wind.** Up here, the wind carries stories from across the city, whispering secrets only heard by those who stand tall against the skyline. It's a reminder of the interconnectedness of the city's life, with each gust a messenger of distant happenings.

➢ **Reflections on the Glass and Steel.** The reflective surfaces of surrounding buildings create a kaleidoscope of images, where the horizon is mirrored and multiplied. In these reflections, the sense of commanding the horizon is amplified, a visual echo of your presence amidst the city's grandeur.

In Commanding the Horizon, the experience is more than just a physical elevation; it's a rise in spirit and ambition. It's about embracing the expanse of Manhattan not just as a backdrop, but as a realm where one's presence resonates with the city's heartbeat, a place where commanding the view symbolizes commanding one's destiny in the vibrant narrative of New York.

Your Triumphs: Commanding the Horizon Activities

Inspirational Quote

HAPPINESS IS NOT BY CHANCE, BUT BY CHOICE. — Jim Rohn

Your Goals: Intentions and Thoughts

Cocktails and Constellations

Cocktails and Constellations encapsulates the enchanting experience of sipping a drink under the night sky on a Manhattan rooftop, where the glittering cityscape meets the celestial wonders above. It's a section that delves into the romance and allure of these elevated moments, blending the sophisticated charm of urban nightlife with the timeless beauty of the stars.

➢ **Sipping Under the Stars**. On a rooftop in Manhattan, cocktails are more than just drinks; they're potions that connect the earthbound revelers to the cosmos. Each sip is a toast to the stars, an acknowledgment of the universe's vastness, mirrored by the city's own twinkling lights.

➢ **The Constellation of Flavors**. Just as stargazers find patterns in the night sky, connoisseurs find a constellation of flavors in their rooftop cocktails. Each drink is a galaxy of taste, a blend of ingredients as carefully crafted as the stars themselves.

➢ **The Skyline's Glow, the Glass's Shimmer**. In the soft illumination of rooftop lights, the cocktails shimmer like liquid jewels. They reflect the city's skyline, creating a visual symphony of colors and lights that enhances the drinking experience.

➢ **Toasting to Aspirations**. As glasses clink against the backdrop of the city, these toasts become more than just celebratory gestures. They're symbols of aspirations and dreams, of the heights one can reach in the city that offers a canvas as vast as the night sky.

➢ **Intimate Conversations Under the Cosmos**. The intimate setting of a rooftop under the open sky, foster conversations that are as deep and expansive as the universe. Here, amidst the whispers and laughter, personal stories and shared dreams weave together, creating bonds as enduring as the constellations.

➢ **The Romance of the Rooftop Night**. There's an inherent romance in these settings, where the beauty of the cosmos meets the allure of the city. It's a perfect backdrop for romantic encounters, where connections are made and love stories begin.

➢ **The Metaphor of Mixing**. The art of mixing a cocktail on a rooftop becomes a metaphor for life in Manhattan—a blend of diverse elements coming together to create something unique, a balance of flavors mirroring the balance of life in the city.

➢ **The Ephemeral Beauty of the Night**. Just like the shifting patterns of stars and planets, the beauty of a rooftop night is ephemeral. Each evening is a unique experience, a fleeting moment of magic that captures the essence of Manhattan's ever-changing nature.

➢ **The Solace in Sipping Solo**. For the solitary drinker, a cocktail under the stars is a moment of solace, a time to reflect and find peace in the midst of the city's chaos, with the sky as a constant, comforting presence.

➢ **Celestial Celebrations**. Rooftop gatherings often turn into celebrations of the celestial—be it a meteor shower, a lunar eclipse, or simply a clear night sky. These events add an extra layer of wonder to the rooftop experience, making each sip of a cocktail a tribute to the marvels of the universe.

In Cocktails and Constellations, the rooftop becomes a space where the earthly delights of a well-crafted drink meet the ethereal beauty of the night sky. It's an episode that celebrates the magic of these moments, where one can savor the flavors of the city while gazing upon the timeless beauty of the stars, all from the unique vantage point of Manhattan's rooftops.

Your Triumphs: Cocktails and Constellations Activities

Inspirational Quote

YOU MUST DO THE THINGS YOU THINK YOU CANNOT DO. — Eleanor Roosevelt

Your Goals: Intentions and Thoughts

Urban Elegance Meets Celestial Dreams

Urban Elegance Meets Celestial Dreams is a poetic exploration of the magical intersection where the sophisticated allure of Manhattan's city life converges with the infinite wonder of the starlit sky. It's a narrative that captures the moments when the glamour of the urban jungle and the mystique of the cosmos dance together in perfect harmony.

➤ **The Tapestry of City Lights and Starry Skies**. This section paints a vivid picture of the Manhattan skyline at night, a glittering tapestry that mirrors the starry heavens above. It's a fusion of earthly splendor and cosmic wonder, where skyscrapers reach for the stars, and the stars seem to descend to the streets.

➤ **Rooftop Realms—Where Dreams Take Flight**. Here, the focus is on the rooftops of Manhattan, elevated sanctuaries where the hustle of city life meets the tranquility of celestial contemplation. These are the stages where dreams are whispered to the night sky, hopes as boundless as the universe.

➤ **The Romance of the Cosmos in the Urban Oasis**. This point delves into the romantic aspect of this convergence, where the backdrop of the city's lights and the vastness of the night sky create a setting ripe for love, enchantment, and intimate connections under the cosmos.

➤ **Reflections on Glass and Steel**. Exploring the reflections of stars and city lights on the glass and steel of Manhattan's buildings, creating a visual symphony that encapsulates the essence of urban elegance meeting celestial dreams. It's a sight that captures the imagination and inspires awe.

➤ **The Night's Whisper in the City's Ear**. This is about the dialogue between the city and the sky. As night falls, it's as if the cosmos whisper secrets to the city, a cosmic conversation that unfolds above the sleepless streets, filled with tales of ancient light and timeless mysteries.

> **Stargazing Amidst Skyscrapers**. In this part, the narrative focuses on the unique experience of stargazing from the heart of the city. Amidst the concrete and neon, glimpses of constellations and celestial bodies remind us of the city's place in the grander scheme of the universe.

> **The Lullaby of the City Night**. Here, the rhythmic pulse of Manhattan at night—the distant sounds of traffic, the gentle buzz of nightlife—becomes a lullaby, a soothing contrast to the silent majesty of the night sky, offering a sense of peace and belonging.

> **Cocktails with the Cosmos**. This point captures the experience of enjoying a nightcap under the stars, where each sip is accompanied by a view of the heavens, merging the luxury of urban nightlife with the ethereal beauty of the night sky.

> **The Solitude of the Urban Astronomer**. For those who find solitude on rooftops or quiet corners of the city, the night sky offers a companion. It's a moment of introspection and wonder, where one can contemplate their place in the universe amidst the city's grandeur.

> **The Dance of Light and Darkness**. Finally, this section explores the interplay of light and darkness in the city at night.

Urban Elegance Meets Celestial Dreams is a celebration of the duality of Manhattan's nature—a bustling metropolis under an ancient, starry sky. It's a testament to the city's ability to inspire and awe, reminding us that even in the midst of urban sophistication, the universe's wonders are always within reach.

Your Triumphs: Dreams of Elegance Activities

Inspirational Quote

ALL OF US NEED TO UNDERSTAND THE IMPORTANCE OF BRANDING. WE
ARE CEOs OF OUR OWN COMPANIES: ME INC. TO BE IN BUSINESS TODAY,
OUR MOST IMPORTANT JOB IS TO BE HEAD MARKETER FOR THE BRAND
CALLED YOU. — Tom Peters in Fast Company

Your Goals: Intentions and Thoughts

The Rooftop Rendezvous as a Metaphor

The Rooftop Rendezvous as a Metaphor delves into the deeper symbolism behind the quintessential Manhattan rooftop experience. It's not merely a social affair or a vantage point; it's a rich metaphor for the aspirations, dreams, and the very essence of life in the city. This narrative thread weaves the physicality of being above the city with the metaphorical rise above life's challenges and the pursuit of something greater.

> ➤ **Ascent Above the Ordinary.** The act of ascending to a rooftop in Manhattan symbolizes rising above the everyday. It's a physical and metaphorical elevation from the mundane, representing an escape from the ordinary and a pursuit of the extraordinary.

> ➤ **The Panoramic Perspective.** From the rooftop, the city is seen in its entirety, offering a perspective that's both literal and figurative. This panoramic view symbolizes the ability to see the "big picture" of life, recognizing opportunities and possibilities that aren't visible from the ground level.

> ➤ **The Sky as a Canvas for Dreams.** The open sky above a rooftop becomes a canvas for dreams and aspirations. Just as the sky holds endless stars and possibilities, the rooftop rendezvous symbolizes the limitless potential of the human spirit and the boundless opportunities that the city offers.

> ➤ **An Oasis of Serenity Amidst Chaos.** Amidst the chaos and noise of the city below, the rooftop offers a serene oasis. This contrast is a metaphor for finding peace and clarity amidst life's challenges, a space to breathe and reflect above the fray.

> ➤ **Intersecting Paths at the Top.** Rooftops bring together people from diverse walks of life, symbolizing the intersection of different paths, ideas, and dreams. It's a reminder of the serendipitous

connections and unexpected opportunities that life in a vibrant city like Manhattan brings.

➤ **Touching the Heights of Ambition**. Being on a rooftop, closer to the sky, symbolizes touching the heights of one's ambition. It reflects the quintessential New York drive to reach for the stars, to achieve one's highest goals and dreams.

➤ **The Night Sky as a Reminder of Humility**. Gazing at the vast night sky from a rooftop can be a humbling experience, a metaphor for recognizing one's place in the universe. It symbolizes the balance of striving for greatness while staying grounded in the reality of our small but significant place in the world.

➤ **The Isolation and Intimacy of Success**. Rooftop gatherings can be intimate, yet they also underscore a sense of isolation that often comes with success or ambition. This duality reflects the Manhattanite's journey of pursuing dreams while navigating the complexities of personal connections.

➤ **The Fragility of the Moment**. The ephemeral nature of a rooftop rendezvous, under the changing sky, symbolizes the fleeting moments of life. It's a metaphor for embracing the present, understanding the transient nature of success, happiness, and life itself.

➤ **The Horizon as a Boundary and a Promise**. It represents the limits of our current reality and the promise of what lies beyond.

In The Rooftop Rendezvous as a Metaphor, each element—the ascent, the view, the sky, the company—is imbued with deeper meaning. It's a reflection of life in Manhattan, where the physical heights mirror the metaphorical peaks of human experience, ambition, and the complex tapestry of urban life.

Your Triumphs: Rooftop Rendezvous' Activities

Inspirational Quote

YOU CAN'T BUILD A REPUTATION ON WHAT YOU ARE GOING TO DO. — Henry Ford

Your Goals: Intentions and Thoughts

Your Goals: Intentions and Thoughts

8

Boutique Brilliance:
Discovering the City's Best-Kept Secrets

Manhattan, a city that's not just a patchwork of buildings and boulevards, but a treasure trove of secrets waiting to be unveiled. Between the grandeur of Fifth Avenue and the pulse of SoHo, lie hidden gems—boutiques that aren't just stores, but portals to worlds of wonder, ambition, and unrivaled style. In this city of a million tales, it's not merely about flaunting big brand names; it's about wearing a narrative, an adventure, a whispered legacy.

Now imagine: You're strolling down an unassuming alley off Tribeca, and there it is—a boutique so chic, so untouched by the masses, that every garment whispers tales of artistry and intrigue. And as you sashay out, eyes aren't just drawn to your unique ensemble, but the story you now wear. That, my dear, is the allure of Boutique Brilliance—a mastery of discovering not just fashion, but soulful tales draped in fabric.

In this captivating chapter of The Manhattan Diaries, we will embark on a journey to the heart of the city's best-kept secrets. From the vintage charm of East Village thrifts to the avant-garde brilliance in Chelsea's nooks, we'll map the routes to fashion's hidden sanctuaries.

But this isn't solely about the thrill of a find—no. It's about the romance of discovery, about resonating with the spirit of designers who pour their dreams and desires into every stitch and seam. It's about that electrifying moment when a piece doesn't just fit your form, but your very essence.

Join me, as we navigate Manhattan's labyrinth, seeking out boutiques that aren't just spaces, but stories, experiences, legacies. Because in this city, every garment is a ticket to a new adventure, a new narrative. Get ready to turn heads, not just with your style, but with the tales you adorn. Welcome to The Manhattan Diaries—where your fashion choices are as enthralling as the city's most whispered legends.

The Hidden Alleys of Fashion Discovery

In the pulsating heart of Manhattan, where the well-trodden paths of Fifth Avenue glisten with the familiar, there lies a more clandestine allure—The Hidden Alleys of Fashion Discovery. These are the city's best-kept secrets, where style is whispered through the winds of the unknown and chic is defined by the bold who dare to venture off the map.

➢ **The Thrill of the Fashion Hunt**. There's a certain thrill, a heartbeat quickening, that comes with the hunt for these hidden fashion sanctuaries. Tucked away in the nooks of Tribeca or nestled in the quaint corners of the East Village, each boutique is a treasure chest waiting to be unlocked, a Pandora's box of style that promises the ecstasy of the unique.

➢ **Discovery Beyond the Doorway**. As you push open the door to one of these elusive boutiques, you're not just stepping into a store; you're entering a realm of imagination. Here, fashion transcends commerce; it's a curation of dreams and a manifestation of the designer's innermost narratives, each garment a page from a diary you never knew existed.

➢ **Echoes of the Designer's Heartbeat**. In these hidden gems, the echo of the designer's heartbeat is palpable. Each piece of clothing hangs not just with elegance but with emotion, imbued with the sweat, tears, and laughter of its creator. Shopping here is an intimate dance with the designer's spirit, a chance to wear a story, to drape oneself in the fabric of their passions and pursuits.

➢ **A Symphony of Textures and Tales**. Running your fingers over the fabrics, you feel the textures of tales untold. Silks whisper secrets of distant lands, while rugged denim shouts of urban adventures. Every thread sewn is a note in a symphony, a harmonious blend of the designer's journey, their triumphs and trials, sewn into seams and hems.

> **The Rendezvous of Rarity and Desire**. In the heart of Manhattan, rarity finds its truest expression in these alcoves of fashion. These boutiques aren't just selling clothes; they are matchmakers of desire and exclusivity, where the rarity of the find makes the heart grow fonder, and the bond between garment and wearer becomes a passionate affair.

> **The Chameleon of Style**. Here, style is a chameleon, ever-evolving, refusing to be pinned down. It's a testament to the city's fashion resilience, where trends are born in the cradle of innovation and individuality reigns supreme. Each boutique visit is an expedition into uncharted territories of style, a journey into the jungles of the avant-garde.

> **The Whispered Legacy of Boutiques**. These hidden boutiques whisper of a legacy, a story of Manhattan that's sewn into the city's very fabric. They are the keepers of fashion's folklore, the custodians of a legacy that is worn, flaunted, and lived.

> **The Fashion Flaneur's Paradise**. For the fashion flaneur, these alleys are a paradise, a labyrinth of style that beckons with the allure of the unknown. It's a world where the act of shopping becomes a journey of self-discovery, a wanderlust of style.

In The Hidden Alleys of Fashion Discovery, every turn down an unmarked path is an invitation to a fashion adventure, a call to those who seek the thrill of the unique and the joy of the discovery. It's an episode that celebrates not just the clothes, but the stories they carry, the dreams they embody, and the indomitable spirit of Manhattan's hidden fashion heart.

Your Triumphs: Fashion Discovery Activities

Inspirational Quote

SOME PEOPLE LOOK FOR A BEAUTIFUL PLACE. OTHERS MAKE A PLACE BEAUTIFUL. — Hazrat Inayat Khan

Your Goals: Intentions and Thoughts

Echoes of the Designer's Dream

In the vibrant tapestry that is Manhattan's fashion scene, Echoes of the Designer's Dream captures the intimate and often unseen narrative woven into the fabric of each garment in the city's hidden boutiques. This is where fashion transcends the realms of threads and textiles, becoming a living, breathing echo of the dreams and aspirations of those who dare to create.

- ➤ **The Whisper of Creation**. Behind every seam and stitch in these quaint boutiques lies the whisper of creation, a story spun from the very soul of the designer. Each piece is not merely crafted; it's born from a cacophony of inspiration, struggle, and triumph, a silent yet eloquent testament to the journey of its creator.

- ➤ **Intimacy in Every Fiber**. Shopping in these hidden gems of Manhattan is an intimate affair. As you glide your fingers over the fabrics, you're not just touching a garment; you're connecting with the heartbeats of dreamers, the hopeful pulse of artists who pour their life's passion into every fiber.

- ➤ **The Canvas of New York**. Each boutique is a canvas where the city's relentless energy and diverse narratives blend into the designer's vision. Here, the chaotic symphony of New York finds harmony in the threads of ambition and creativity, each design a tribute to the city's relentless drive.

- ➤ **Fashion as a Personal Diary**. For the designers behind these boutique windows, fashion is their diary, a personal chronicle of their evolution. Every collection tells a story, a chapter of their lives rendered in fabric and color, waiting to be read by those who seek more than just attire.

- ➤ **The Legacy of the Stitch**. In these boutiques, every stitch carries a legacy. It's a legacy of late nights, early mornings, joys, and setbacks.

The designers leave bits of their history in every hem and fold, crafting not just clothes but heirlooms of their perseverance and creativity.

➤ **A Dialogue with the Wearer**. Each creation initiates a silent dialogue with its wearer. It's a conversation about style, identity, and the unspoken bond that forms when someone chooses to wear a piece that resonates with their own story, a fusion of the designer's dream and the wearer's narrative.

➤ **The Alchemy of Design**. In the heart of Manhattan, design becomes alchemy. It's where raw materials are transformed into expressions of identity and artistry. These boutiques stand as altars to this alchemy, spaces where the mundane is turned into the magical.

➤ **The Symphony of the Unseen**. Echoes of the Designer's Dream is a symphony of the unseen, a celebration of the myriad untold stories that culminate in the creation of a fashion piece. It's a homage to the invisible threads that connect the designer's vision with the city's heartbeat.

➤ **The Resonance of Timeless Tales**. In the final narrative herein, we find that each boutique piece in Manhattan is not just a momentary trend, but a resonance of timeless tales. These creations stand as sartorial storytellers, echoing the past, embracing the present, and envisioning the future.

In Echoes of the Designer's Dream, every garment is a narrative, a piece of a dream made tangible. It's a journey into the heart of Manhattan's fashion soul, a voyage that uncovers the profound connections between creator, creation, and wearer. In this city, fashion is more than what meets the eye; it's a resonance of dreams woven into the very fabric of Manhattan.

Your Triumphs: Designer's Dream Activities

_____

_____

_____

_____

_____

_____

_____

_____

_____

_____

_____

_____

_____

_____

_____

_____

_____

_____

_____

_____

_____

_____

_____

_____

_____

_____

Inspirational Quote

TOO MANY PEOPLE OVERVALUE WHAT THEY ARE NOT AND UNDERVALUE WHAT THEY ARE . — Malcom Forbes

Your Goals: Intentions and Thoughts

Fashion as a Narrative

In the whirlwind that is Manhattan, where style is as much a language as it is an adornment, Fashion as a Narrative delves into the enchanting story behind every hem, every drape, every carefully chosen accessory. Here, in the city that's always ahead of the curve, fashion isn't just about what you wear; it's about the story you choose to tell the world.

- ➤ **Wearing a Story, Not Just a Dress**. As you glide through the streets of Manhattan, each outfit is a chapter of your own personal narrative. The silk scarf from a hidden boutique whispers of a romantic escapade, the vintage boots speak of edgy adventures on the Lower East Side. Fashion here isn't mere clothing; it's a mosaic of your experiences, a sartorial autobiography.

- ➤ **The Dialogue of Style**. Every fashion choice is a sentence, a paragraph, a dialogue with the world. The bold print of a dress, the understated elegance of a classic coat, each speaks volumes. In Manhattan, your style is your voice before you even say a word, a prelude to the story you're about to tell.

- ➤ **The Evolution of Personal Fashion Tales**. Just as every New Yorker's journey is dynamic, so too is their fashion narrative. It's an ever-evolving tale, from the experimental phases of youth to the refined choices of maturity. Each phase of life adds depth to your wardrobe's story, each piece a symbol of growth, a marker of change.

- ➤ **The Intimacy of Garment and Wearer**. In the city's plethora of boutiques and ateliers, finding a piece that resonates with you creates an intimate bond. It's the magic of discovering something that feels like it was made just for you, a garment that understands your story, ready to be woven into the fabric of your life.

- ➢ **Fashion as a Time Capsule**. Each ensemble is a time capsule, capturing the essence of a moment, a mood, an era. The flapper dress from a vintage store in Chelsea takes you back to the Roaring Twenties, while a cutting-edge piece from a SoHo designer propels you into the future. Fashion in Manhattan is a journey through time, with each outfit a ticket to a different era.

- ➢ **The Synchronicity with the City's Pulse**. Your fashion narrative is in sync with the pulse of the city. The vibrant, eclectic energy of Manhattan is mirrored in the colors, textures, and styles that adorn its inhabitants. Just as the city never sleeps, your fashion story is continuously unfolding, a living, breathing entity.

- ➢ **The Fashion Icon's Journey**. For the fashion-forward, this narrative is not just about following trends; it's about being a trendsetter. It's about pioneering a style that's all your own, leading the way in a city that's always on the cutting edge of what's next.

- ➢ **The Unspoken Conversations of Style**. In Manhattan's grand tapestry of fashion, each outfit sparks an unspoken conversation, a silent discourse that speaks to the observer and the observed. It's in the nuances of your attire where dialogues are held without words, where a glance at a particularly daring ensemble or a nod to a classic look becomes a shared moment of appreciation. In this city, fashion is a language unto itself, a means of connection that transcends the spoken word, weaving a web of silent narratives between strangers who share nothing but a moment and a mutual recognition of style.

In Fashion as a Narrative, every thread, every fabric, every ensemble is part of a larger story, the story of you, set against the backdrop of the most dynamic city in the world. It's about embracing fashion as a form of self-expression, a way to tell your tale in a city that celebrates individuality, creativity, and the endless possibilities of style.

Your Triumphs: Your Fashion Narrative Activities

Inspirational Quote

IT IS OUR ATTITUDE AT THE BEGINNING OF A DIFFICULT TASK, WHICH MORE THAN ANYTHING ELSE, WILL AFFECT ITS SUCCESSFUL OUTCOME. — William James

Your Goals: Intentions and Thoughts

The Legacy of Boutique Brilliance

In the luminous streets of Manhattan, where every corner has its own rhythm and every building its own story, The Legacy of Boutique Brilliance captures the essence of what it means to be both timeless and timely in fashion. This narrative isn't just about the clothes we drape ourselves in; it's about the enduring legacy we weave through our choices, the indelible mark we leave in the city through our style.

➢ **Beyond the Momentary Glitter**. In the heart of Manhattan, boutique brilliance is not just a fleeting sparkle; it's a lasting glow. It's about finding pieces that defy the ephemeral trends, garments that carry the weight and beauty of a story that continues to resonate through time.

➢ **The Heirlooms of Tomorrow**. These boutiques don't just sell clothes; they curate future heirlooms. The lace dress, the hand-stitched leather bag, the bespoke suit—each is destined to become a cherished token, passed down through generations, whispering tales of Manhattan nights and days.

➢ **A Tapestry Woven with Stories**. Each boutique in Manhattan is a thread in a grander tapestry, a narrative of a city that's as much about its future as it is about its storied past. The legacy of boutique brilliance is in how these threads intertwine, creating a fabric rich with history and promise.

➢ **The Romance of timelessness**. There's a romance in the timelessness that these boutiques offer. In a city that's always rushing towards the next big thing, these spaces offer a pause, a reminder that true style is beyond time, a constant in the ever-changing world of fashion.

➢ **The Signature of the City**. Boutique brilliance is Manhattan's signature, a stamp of individuality and sophistication. It's in the unique finds from a small shop in Greenwich Village, the avant-garde piece from an up-and-coming designer in SoHo—each a reflection of the city's eclectic spirit.

➢ **Crafting Personal Histories**. Shopping in these boutiques is about crafting your personal history, about adding chapters to your narrative through pieces that speak not just to trends but to your journey, your identity, and your place in the tapestry of the city.

➢ **The Whisper of Elegance in the Urban Jungle**. Amidst the city's relentless pace, boutique brilliance is a whisper of elegance, a soft but powerful presence. It's a reminder that amidst the steel and concrete, the heart of Manhattan beats in silk, leather, and linen, in the timeless elegance of carefully crafted fashion.

➢ **The Reflection of a Changing Cityscape**. As Manhattan evolves, these boutiques reflect the changing cityscape in their windows. They adapt, grow, and transform, yet their essence remains rooted in a tradition of quality and exclusivity. The legacy of boutique brilliance is not just in maintaining the past but in evolving with the city's heartbeat, in being a part of its continuous reinvention while holding onto the timeless allure of personal, curated fashion.

In The Legacy of Boutique Brilliance, every purchase, every choice, is an act of defiance against the ephemeral, a declaration of the enduring power of style. It's a narrative that celebrates not just the beauty of the present but the allure of a legacy, the kind that's sewn into the very fabric of Manhattan, forever chic, forever elegant, forever New York.

Your Triumphs: Boutique Brilliance Activities

Inspirational Quote

HAPPINESS OFTEN SNEAKS IN THROUGH A DOOR YOU DIDN'T KNOW YOU LEFT OPEN. — John Barrymore

Your Goals: Intentions and Thoughts

Stepping Into Your Own Stilettos – The Art of Self-Coaching

In the glittering constellation that is Manhattan, where ambition dances in the eyes of its inhabitants, Stepping Into Your Own Stilettos—The Art of Self-Coaching is a declaration of independence, a siren song to the soul. It's not just about strutting in designer heels; it's about the empowering journey of carving your own path, the art of coaching yourself to become the leading lady in the grand drama of your life.

➢ **The First Step in High Heels**. Picture this: a pair of stilettos, not just as footwear but as a symbol of strength. Slipping into them is the first step of self-coaching, a physical manifestation of stepping into your power, your confidence. It's about embracing the click-clack on the pavement as your personal soundtrack, a rhythm of empowerment.

➢ **Mirror Conversations**. In the quiet of your apartment, with the city's lights as your backdrop, the mirror becomes your confidante. Here, you coach yourself, practicing the art of positive self-talk, affirming your dreams, your goals, your worth. It's about looking yourself in the eye and recognizing the star you are.

➢ **Navigating the City's Highs and Lows**. Just as Manhattan is a terrain of ups and downs, so too is the journey of self-coaching. It's about learning to navigate through the setbacks with grace, to celebrate the victories with humility. Each step, each stumble, in those stilettos is a lesson in resilience, a testament to your tenacity.

➢ **The Cocktail of Confidence**. Imagine sipping on confidence like it's your favorite cocktail. Self-coaching is about mixing the ingredients of courage, wisdom, and self-belief, garnishing it with a twist of sass. It's a drink you serve yourself daily, a reminder of your capabilities.

➤ **The Whisper of Self-Encouragement**. In the hustle of the city, the most crucial voice is the one that comes from within. It's the gentle whisper of self-encouragement when doubts loom, the roaring cheer during moments of triumph. Learning the language of self-support is the essence of self-coaching.

➤ **The Runway of Life**. View Manhattan as your runway, a place where every day is an opportunity to showcase your style, your personality, your essence. Self-coaching is about strutting down this runway with confidence, turning heads not just with your fashion sense but with the aura of self-assuredness you exude.

➤ **Reflections in Rain Puddles**. On rainy days, when puddles line the streets, see them not as obstacles but as mirrors reflecting your journey. They are reminders of the importance of self-reflection in self-coaching, of looking at your path, acknowledging your progress, and adjusting your stride.

➤ **The Dance of Independence**. Self-coaching is a dance of independence. It's about moving to your own rhythm, not being swayed by the city's frenetic pace. It's a dance where you lead, where you choose the music, the steps, the direction.

➤ **The Sparkle of Self-Discovery**. Like the city at night, self-coaching is about discovering your sparkle, your unique light. It's about illuminating the corners of your personality, embracing your quirks, your strengths, your essence, and letting them shine brightly in the city of lights.

In Stepping Into Your Own Stilettos—The Art of Self-Coaching, it's not just about walking confidently; it's about walking consciously, with purpose, passion, and a pinch of Manhattan panache. It's a journey of self-discovery, of finding your place in the city and the world, one empowered step at a time.

Your Triumphs: Self-Coaching Activities

_____

Inspirational Quote

LIFE CHANGES VERY QUICKLY; IN A VERY POSITIVE WAY, IF YOU LET IT. —
Lindsey Vonn

Your Goals: Intentions and Thoughts

Your Goals: Intentions and Thoughts

9

Dinner Dates and Late-Night Fates:
Manhattan's Recipe for Unforgettable Evenings

Manhattan, a city that doesn't merely indulge in dinner dates—it feasts on them, as every clink of a glass and shared glance across the table pulses with tales of intrigue, possibility, and the thrill of the unknown. In this metropolis of magic, it's not simply about choosing a restaurant; it's about curating an experience, a moment suspended between the twilight and dawn, where destinies intertwine and stories take flight.

Now imagine: You're navigating the cobbled streets of Greenwich Village, the glint of old-world lanterns illuminating your path. Every gaze that meets yours isn't just smitten by your ensemble, but the promise of a night drenched in allure and mystique. That, my darling, is Manhattan's Dance of dining and dreaming, a ballet where every movement, every gesture is an invitation to a world of wonder and whispers.

In this tantalizing chapter of The Manhattan Diaries, we'll embark on an odyssey of the senses. From the enchanting hideaways of Upper East Side where old money meets timeless charm, to the pulsating eateries of the Meatpacking District, where the modern and the historic seductively entwine, you'll learn the art of orchestrating evenings that don't just satisfy the palate but stir the soul.

But this journey isn't merely about flavors and aromas—no. It's about the intoxication of connection, the allure of shared secrets under the soft glow of chandeliers. It's about understanding that in Manhattan, dining isn't just a meal, it's a performance, a play of passions and possibilities.

Join me, as we delve deep into the city's culinary theatres and moonlit alcoves, crafting narratives that don't just end with dessert, but linger, long into the night. Because in Manhattan, every dinner date is an overture to an epic. Fasten your seatbelt and sharpen your appetite, for the city is set to serve you an experience like no other. Welcome to The Manhattan Diaries—where your evening escapades can become the stuff of legend.

The Enchantment of Location Selection

In the mesmerizing mosaic that is Manhattan, where every street sings a different melody and every neighborhood tells its own tale, The Enchantment of Location Selection is the first act in the art of crafting an unforgettable evening. It's not merely about picking a restaurant; it's about choosing a stage for the night's unfolding drama, a place where the ambiance whispers as loudly as the conversation, where the setting is as crucial to the plot as the characters themselves.

- ➤ **Romancing the Streets of SoHo**. Imagine wandering through the cobbled streets of SoHo, where each restaurant and bistro is imbued with an air of bohemian chic, a perfect setting for a rendezvous that's as stylish as it is intimate. The ambiance here is a blend of the trendy and the timeless, setting the stage for an evening where romance is scripted in every brick and pane.

- ➤ **Upper East Side Elegance**. Step into the Upper East Side, where the dining establishments exude an air of refined elegance. Here, selecting a location is like choosing a chapter from an F. Scott Fitzgerald novel, a backdrop of old-world charm and sophistication, perfect for a night where conversations sparkle as brightly as the champagne.

- ➤ **The Vibrancy of the Village**. In the heart of Greenwich Village, the selection of a locale comes with an undercurrent of artistic history and cultural richness. It's where the tables tell tales of poets and painters, and the walls are lined with the echoes of jazz and laughter, a place for those who desire their evenings infused with a touch of the bohemian spirit.

➤ **The Charm of Chelsea's Hidden Gems**. In the artistic alleys of Chelsea, location selection becomes an exploration of culinary innovation and intimate charm. Here, each dining spot is a hidden gem, a secret waiting to be shared. Whether it's a cozy farm-to-table experience or a chic eatery boasting avant-garde cuisine, choosing a spot in Chelsea is for those evenings when you desire your meal served with a side of artistic flair and understated sophistication.

➤ **The Rooftop Rendezvous of Midtown**. Ascend to the rooftop dining spots of Midtown, where the city's skyline serves as your backdrop, twinkling with a million lights.

➤ **Downtown's Daring Culinary Scenes**. Venture further downtown, and the choices become edgier, more avant-garde. Here, selecting a spot is for the bold, for those who seek to marry fine dining with an adrenaline rush, where the plates are as daring as the palates, and the settings as unconventional as the experiences they promise.

➤ **The Theater District's Dramatic Flair**. Near Broadway, the restaurants are stages themselves, each offering a prelude to the night's main act. Choosing a location here means immersing yourself in the dramatic, in spaces where the energy of the nearby stages spills over into every corner, setting the scene for an evening where you're both audience and star.

In The Enchantment of Location Selection, every choice of venue in Manhattan is a chapter in a grander narrative, an opening scene to an evening that promises to be as thrilling as the city itself. It's about understanding that in this city, the backdrop is integral to the story, and where you dine can define the entire arc of your night. This is Manhattan, where every dinner date is an opportunity to step into a story, to be a character in a setting that's as enchanting as the tales it inspires.

Your Triumphs: Stepping Into Your Story Activities

Inspirational Quote

AS I GROW OLDER, I PAY LESS ATTENTION TO WHAT MEN SAY. I JUST WATCH WHAT THEY DO. — Andrew Carnegie

DINNER DATES AND LATE-NIGHT FATES

Your Goals: Intentions and Thoughts

Culinary Couture—Dressing for the Occasion

In the dazzling kaleidoscope that is Manhattan's dining scene, Culinary Couture—Dressing for the Occasion is not just about adorning oneself for a dinner date; it's about donning an ensemble that echoes the evening's promise. This episode of The Manhattan Diaries is a sartorial serenade to the city, where each outfit is a careful composition, a blend of fabric and fantasy, tailored to the night's culinary script.

- ➢ **The Fabric of the Evening**. Every dinner date in Manhattan calls for a costume as carefully curated as the menu. It's about choosing an ensemble that speaks to the soul of the restaurant, be it the understated elegance for a Michelin-starred marvel or the eclectic chic for a trendy downtown bistro. Your attire sets the tone, a prelude to the evening's culinary symphony.

- ➢ **Accessorizing for Ambiance**. Imagine selecting accessories that aren't just ornaments but conversation starters, pieces that catch the light and the eye, mirroring the ambiance of your chosen eatery. In Manhattan, a statement necklace or a dapper pocket square can be the spice that completes the evening's ensemble.

- ➢ **The Silhouette of Style and Cuisine**. In the art of dressing for dinner, it's about creating a silhouette that complements the cuisine. A sleek, modern cut for a fusion restaurant, or a flowy, romantic dress for an intimate Italian trattoria. Each choice is a nod to the culinary experience, a visual appetizer to the feast.

- ➢ **The Palette of the Plate and the Wardrobe**. Consider the color palette of your outfit as an extension of the dining experience. A pop of color for a vibrant tapas place, or muted, sophisticated tones for a classic French bistro. It's about harmonizing your wardrobe with the flavors and colors of the food, a blend of taste and style.

➤ **Heels, Flats, and Culinary Paths**. The choice of footwear is a dance with the evening's itinerary. Stilettos might lead you down the path of opulence and flair, while chic flats could guide you through a casual, yet charming culinary adventure. In Manhattan, your shoes can dictate the rhythm of the night.

➤ **The Whisper of Textiles and Tastes**. It's about dressing in a way that your outfit hums in harmony with the culinary tunes of the night.

➤ **The Alchemy of Mood and Mode**. In the heart of Manhattan, your fashion choice is an alchemy that blends mood with mode. A rooftop dinner under the stars calls for a touch of sparkle, a garment that catches the night sky's glimmer, while a cozy, candlelit corner in a downtown eatery invites the warmth of velvet or the softness of cashmere. Your outfit becomes a sensory extension of the dining experience, a tangible expression of the evening's ambiance.

➤ **The Finishing Touch of Confidence**. The final ingredient in Culinary Couture is an intangible yet essential one—confidence. In Manhattan, the most striking accessory you can don is the air of self-assuredness. It's about stepping into the dining scene with the poise of someone who knows they're not just dressed for the occasion, but dressed to conquer it, turning heads not just for the clothes they wear, but for the way they wear them.

In Culinary Couture—Dressing for the Occasion, every thread, every fabric choice is a testament to the city's fashion-forward heartbeat. It's a narrative that celebrates the union of style and taste, where dressing for dinner is an ode to the city's culinary and fashion landscape. This episode isn't just about looking good; it's about feeling in tune with the city's rhythm, about wearing an outfit that's not just seen but savored, much like the exquisite dining experiences Manhattan has to offer.

Your Triumphs: Culinary Couture Activities

Inspirational Quote

INSPIRATION IS SOME MYSTERIOUS BLESSING, WHICH HAPPENS WHEN THE WHEELS ARE TURNING SMOOTHLY. — Quentin Blake

DINNER DATES AND LATE-NIGHT FATES

Your Goals: Intentions and Thoughts

A Symphony of Flavors and Feelings

In the rhythmic heart of Manhattan, where every bite tells a story and every sip sings a song, A Symphony of Flavors and Feelings is not just about dining; it's about embarking on a sensory journey. Here, in the city that never sleeps, dinner dates transform into a melodious affair, where the clatter of cutlery and the murmur of conversations blend into a symphony as rich and varied as the city itself.

- ➤ **The Overture of Appetizers**. The evening begins with an overture of appetizers, each a prelude to the culinary narrative ahead. It's a flirtatious start, a playful tease of the palate, where flavors mingle and dance, setting the stage for the story that's about to unfold.

- ➤ **The Crescendo of the Main Course**. As the main course arrives, it's a crescendo of tastes and textures. Each dish is a harmonious composition, a careful balance of ingredients and seasonings that sing to your soul. It's about savoring every note, every nuance of flavor, as it resonates with your own emotions and memories.

- ➤ **The Intimacy of Shared Plates**. There's an intimacy in sharing plates, a gesture that weaves a bond between diners. It's a delicate dance of give and take, a sharing of tastes that becomes a sharing of stories and laughter, a mingling of spirits in the candlelit ambience of Manhattan's dining rooms.

- ➤ **The Interlude of Interactions**. In between bites, the interactions at the table are their own melody. The clinking of glasses in a toast, the meeting of eyes across the table, the subtle brush of hands as dishes are passed—each a note in the evening's score, each adding depth to the dining experience.

> **The Finale of Desserts and Digestifs**. As the meal draws to a close, the dessert and digestifs arrive like a final act. It's a sweet, lingering finale, a moment to savor the aftertaste of both the food and the company, a chance to bask in the afterglow of an evening spent in gastronomic and emotional indulgence.

> **The Duet of Wine and Ambiance**. In this symphony, the choice of wine is a duet with the ambiance. The velvety caress of a rich red in a dimly lit, romantic setting, or the playful sparkle of a white in a vibrant, upbeat bistro—each pairing is a dance of senses, a harmonious blend that elevates both the drink and the moment.

> **The Solo of Signature Dishes**. Every restaurant in Manhattan has its signature dish, a solo performance in the evening's symphony. It's a standout piece, a burst of culinary creativity that captures the essence of the chef's artistry, leaving an imprint not just on the palate but in the memory, a lingering melody of taste.

> **The Encore of Evening Strolls**. Often, the symphony extends beyond the restaurant's walls. A post-dinner stroll through Manhattan's streets becomes an encore, a time to digest both the meal and the night's conversations. The city's lights, sounds, and energy compose a background score, adding layers to the evening's experience, turning a simple walk into a continuation of the night's harmony.

In A Symphony of Flavors and Feelings, every dinner date in Manhattan is an orchestration of the senses. It's an episode that celebrates the city's culinary artistry, not just as a feast for the palate but as a concert for the heart. It's about understanding that in this city, a meal is never just a meal; it's a journey through a landscape of flavors and emotions, a journey that leaves you both sated and yearning for more.

Your Triumphs: Flavors and Feelings Activities

Inspirational Quote

DON'T BE SCARED TO PRESENT THE REAL YOU TO THE WORLD, AUTHENTICITY IS AT THE HEART OF SUCCESS. — Unknown

DINNER DATES AND LATE-NIGHT FATES

Your Goals: Intentions and Thoughts

The Intimacy of Shared Plates and Conversations

In the city that's a mosaic of lights and dreams, The Intimacy of Shared Plates and Conversations is an episode that delves into the heart of Manhattan's dining experience. It's where the clatter of the city fades into a soft hum, and the tables become islands of intimacy, illuminated by the flicker of candlelight and the warmth of shared stories.

➤ **The Dance of the Shared Plate**. There's an unspoken ballet in the act of sharing a plate. It's a dance of give and take, a rhythm set to the tune of "try this, taste that." In this dance, each dish is more than a culinary delight; it's an expression of trust, an invitation to enter one's personal taste world, a gesture that says, "I want to share more than just a meal with you."

➤ **Conversations Seasoned with Laughter and Insight**. As the plates circulate, so do the conversations, seasoned with laughter, sprinkled with insights. In these shared moments, dialogues unfold naturally, stories are passed around like cherished dishes, and the intimacy of the experience deepens with each bite, each revelation.

➤ **The Serendipity of Flavorful Discoveries**. In the sharing of plates, there's a serendipity of discovery. You might find yourself enchanted by a flavor you never thought to try, a testament to the adventurous spirit of Manhattan dining. It's about opening up to new experiences, both in taste and in tales.

➤ **The Art of Savoring Together**. Sharing a meal is about savoring together, syncing your culinary rhythm with that of your dining companion. It's in the mutual nods of approval, the shared smiles of satisfaction, that the meal becomes a joint venture, a shared journey of the palate and the heart.

- ➢ **A Tapestry of Tastes and Tales**. Every shared plate weaves a tapestry of tastes and tales. It's a canvas painted with the colors of different cuisines, each brushstroke a different dish, each hue a different flavor, coming together to create a masterpiece of culinary and conversational art.

- ➢ **The Whisper of Shared Secrets**. In the close quarters of Manhattan's cozy eateries, shared plates lead to shared secrets. The intimacy of the setting encourages a lowering of guards, where conversations flow more freely, turning from casual banter to heartfelt confessions. It's in these moments that bonds are strengthened, and new depths of relationships are explored.

- ➢ **A Canvas for Culinary Adventure**. Sharing plates in Manhattan is about painting a canvas of culinary adventure. It's an opportunity to experiment with diverse cuisines, a chance to step out of comfort zones together. Each dish becomes a new chapter in the evening's story, each flavor a new twist in the tale.

- ➢ **The Last Bite—A Moment of Reflection**. As the meal draws to a close, the last bite becomes a moment of reflection. It's a time to savor not just the flavors but the company and the conversation. This final shared morsel is often a bittersweet moment, a symbol of an experience that will soon become a cherished memory.

In The Intimacy of Shared Plates and Conversations, Manhattan's dining scene is more than a collection of restaurants; it's a stage for connection, a realm where the sharing of a meal becomes an act of intimacy, a communion of flavors and stories. It's a celebration of the bonds that are formed over shared plates, the friendships deepened, the romances kindled, all set against the backdrop of the city's vibrant culinary tapestry.

Your Triumphs: Shared Intimacy Activities

Inspirational Quote

WITH THE RIGHT KIND OF COACHING AND DETERMINATION, YOU CAN ACCOMPLISH ANYTHING. — Reese Witherspoon

DINNER DATES AND LATE-NIGHT FATES

Your Goals: Intentions and Thoughts

The Unwritten Epilogue of the Night

In the city that's always scripting its next act, The Unwritten Epilogue of the Night is a whispered invitation to the unknown, a seductive promise that the end of a Manhattan dinner date is merely the beginning of a new adventure. It's in these twilight hours, as the last plates are cleared and the candles flicker low, that the true magic of the city begins to unveil itself.

➤ **The Anticipation of the Unknown**. As dinner winds down, there's a palpable sense of anticipation, a collective holding of breath for what might come next. It's the thrill of the unknown, the allure of the unplanned. In Manhattan, the night's epilogue is unwritten, teeming with potential and possibility.

➤ **The Serendipity of Post-Dinner Wanderings**. Often, the most memorable part of the evening is the part that's unplanned. A spontaneous walk through the moonlit streets of the West Village, an impromptu visit to a jazz club in Harlem, or a shared cab ride to a riverside vista for a view of the skyline—these post-dinner wanderings are where connections deepen and stories unfold.

➤ **A Dance with Destiny**. In the city that never sleeps, each step after dinner can be a dance with destiny. You might find yourself drawn into a late-night gallery opening, a rooftop party, or a quiet bench conversation in Central Park. It's in these moments that the night's true epilogue is written, not with pen and paper, but with footsteps and heartbeats.

➤ **The Whisper of Possibility in the Air**. As you step out of the restaurant, there's a whisper of possibility in the air, a sense of adventure that hangs amidst the city's skyscrapers and stars. It's a call to embrace the spontaneity that Manhattan offers, a reminder that the night is still young and ripe with potential.

> **The Lasting Embrace of the Evening**. When the night finally draws to a close, whether it ends with a tender goodbye on a street corner or a promise of another rendezvous, it leaves an indelible mark. The unwritten epilogue of the night lingers, a sweet, lingering embrace that stays with you long after the city's lights have dimmed.

> **The Allure of Late-Night New York**. After dark, the streets of Manhattan come alive. It's in these late hours that the city reveals its true colors—an impromptu invitation to a hidden speakeasy, a last-minute decision to catch a late-night comedy show, or simply wandering through the city's glowing avenues, where every step is a brushstroke in the night's canvas.

> **The Intimacy of Moonlit Reflections**. There's an intimacy found in the quiet corners of Manhattan after dark, away from the hustle and bustle. A bench by the East River offers a moment of reflection under the moonlight, a chance to share thoughts and dreams in the serenity of the city's softer side, where the water's gentle lapping accompanies confessions and promises.

> **The Last Dance of the Evening**. As the night winds down, there might be a final stop—a late-night dance at a rooftop bar or a quiet moment in a 24-hour diner, sipping coffee and recounting the evening's adventures. It's in its final hours that the night's epilogue is truly penned, not in words, but in shared glances and smiles, in the silent acknowledgment that the evening has been one to remember.

In The Unwritten Epilogue of the Night, every dinner date in Manhattan is an opening chapter to a story yet to be told, a story that extends beyond the confines of a dining table, out into the streets and into the heart of the city. It's an ode to the unexpected, to the moments that can't be planned or predicted, to the magic that unfolds when you allow the city to take the lead and guide you through its nocturnal ballet.

Your Triumphs: Whispered Invitations Activities

Inspirational Quote

PERSONAL BRANDING IS ABOUT MANAGING YOUR NAME—EVEN IF YOU DON'T OWN A BUSINESS—IN A WORLD OF MISINFORMATION, DISINFORMATION, AND SEMI-PERMANENT GOOGLE RECORDS. GOING ON A DATE? CHANCES ARE THAT YOUR "BLIND" DATE HAS GOOGLED YOUR NAME. GOING TO A JOB INTERVIEW? DITTO. — Tim Ferriss

DINNER DATES AND LATE-NIGHT FATES

Your Goals: Intentions and Thoughts

Your Goals: Intentions and Thoughts

Endings that Echo: Ensuring Your Exit Is as Memorable as Your Entrance

Manhattan, a city that doesn't merely applaud the entrance—it's enraptured by the exit, as every farewell whispers tales of allure, enigma, and a promise of return. In this city of infinite stories and spectacles, leaving isn't just about saying goodbye; it's about ensuring that every memory lingers, leaving an indelible mark on the tapestry of the night.

Now imagine: You're departing an Upper East Side soiree, the glow of city lights painting a halo around you. The onlookers aren't just captivated by the elegance of your silhouette, but by the mystique of your departure, a grand finale to a night of revelry and romance. That, my darling, is Manhattan's Grand Adieu, a subtle art form that reminds the city of your irreplaceable presence, ensuring your absence is felt long after you've vanished beyond the horizon.

In this tantalizing chapter of The Manhattan Diaries, we'll delve into the nuances of the perfect farewell. From the lingering touch of a gloved hand waving from the back of a cab to the enigmatic smile that promises a reunion, you'll master the art of leaving an impression that's as lasting as the city itself.

But this isn't just about theatrics—no. It's about understanding the heartbeats and harmonies of Manhattan, ensuring your goodbye becomes a hauntingly beautiful melody that beckons and bewitches. It's about making sure that while endings are inevitable, they are also unforgettable, echoing through the canyons of the city and the chambers of the heart.

Join me, as we chart the course of spectacular farewells and encore-worthy exits, crafting departures that don't merely signify an end but herald the promise of another enchanting beginning. Because in Manhattan, every ending is an invitation for another rendezvous. Tighten your stilettos and let your aura shimmer, for the city is eager for your encore. Welcome to The Manhattan Diaries—where your exit is as breathtaking as your arrival.

The Art of the Graceful Goodbye

In the luminous labyrinth of Manhattan, where every encounter is a scene from an unwritten screenplay, The Art of the Graceful Goodbye is the final act of an evening's performance. It's about leaving with the same flair and finesse that marked your arrival, ensuring that your departure is as much a part of the night's narrative as your entrance was.

- ➢ **The Ballet of the Farewell**. Picture yourself at the end of a sparkling soiree, your exit is not just a departure; it's a ballet. Every step, every gesture, is a move in a carefully choreographed dance. The way you drift from the crowd, the gentle sweep of your hand, the soft, yet poignant smile you offer—it's a performance that captivates, leaving a trail of wistful glances in your wake.

- ➢ **Whispers of the Next Chapter**. The graceful goodbye is punctuated with whispers that hint at future stories. It's about leaving on a note of mystery and promise, dropping subtle cues of "Until next time." It's a whispered "See you soon" that lingers in the air, tantalizing suggestion that this is not an ending, but a pause in a continuing tale.

- ➢ **The Elegance of Poise Under the Spotlight**. In Manhattan, farewells are often under the watchful gaze of an audience. Your goodbye is about maintaining elegance under this spotlight. It's the poise with which you retrieve your coat, the graceful nod to the host, the effortless way you glide through the door—each a portrait of composure and confidence.

- ➢ **The Lasting Echo of Your Departure**. As you step out into the cool Manhattan night, your exit leaves an echo, a lingering sense of your presence. It's in the way people continue to speak of you after you've left, the ripple of your absence that stirs a sense of anticipation for your next appearance.

➤ **The Subtlety of the Exit Timing**. In the art of the graceful goodbye, timing is everything. It's about knowing when to make your exit—not too early to seem disinterested, but not too late to overstay your welcome. The perfect departure is a balancing act, leaving at the high point of the evening, preserving the night's allure and your mystique.

➤ **The Signature Send-off Gesture**. Cultivate a signature gesture that marks your farewells—it could be a certain way of waving, a playful wink, or a warm, lingering handshake. This personal touch becomes synonymous with your persona, a memorable trait that sets your goodbyes apart, making them uniquely yours.

➤ **The Encore in Your Eyes**. As you bid your adieus, let your eyes do the talking. A lingering, meaningful glance can convey a multitude of unsaid thoughts—gratitude for the evening, the pleasure of company, the silent promise of future encounters. It's about leaving an impression that's not just felt but seen.

➤ **The Whisper of Your Fragrance**. A subtle yet powerful element of your goodbye is the lingering scent of your perfume or cologne. It should be a gentle whisper, not an overwhelming shout, leaving a trace of your presence that lingers in the room long after you've departed, a sensory reminder of your elegance and poise.

In The Art of the Graceful Goodbye, it's about understanding that in the grand theatre of Manhattan, every exit is as important as an entrance. It's about ensuring that your departure is not just a moment of leaving, but a lasting impression, a final brushstroke on the evening's canvas that leaves them yearning for your return. It's a reminder that in the city of endless beginnings, the art of the goodbye is just another scene in your ongoing Manhattan story.

Your Triumphs: The Graceful Goodbye Activities

Inspirational Quote

KEEP YOUR FACE ALWAYS TOWARD THE SUNSHINE, AND SHADOWS WILL FALL BEHIND YOU. — Walt Whitman

Your Goals: Intentions and Thoughts

Lasting Impressions in Parting Words

In the tapestry of Manhattan's nights, where every conversation is a thread of gold, Lasting Impressions in Parting Words is about weaving a final strand that glimmers long after you've departed. It's the art of leaving behind words that linger in the air like a melody, a sweet serenade that echoes in the minds and hearts of those you leave behind.

- ➢ **The Poetry of Goodbye**. Your parting words are not just phrases; they are poetry. Craft them with care and charm. A well-placed complement, a witty remark, a heartfelt thank you—each word should be chosen for its ability to resonate, to stay with your audience like the refrain of a beloved song.

- ➢ **The Promise of Future Tales**. As you bid farewell, infuse your words with the promise of future stories. It's about leaving a hint of adventures yet to be had, of tales yet to be told. Your goodbye should be a door left ajar, an invitation to the next chapter, a subtle suggestion that the best is yet to come.

- ➢ **The Elegance of Eloquence**. In Manhattan, where eloquence is as admired as the skyline, your farewell should be as stylish as your ensemble. It's about being memorable for your wit and warmth, about crafting a goodbye that's as sophisticated as it is sincere.

- ➢ **The Whisper of Mystery**. Your last words should also have a whisper of mystery, a hint of the enigmatic. They should leave your company wondering, pondering the depths behind your smile, the stories behind your eyes. It's about creating an allure that invites curiosity and admiration.

- ➢ **A Toast to Shared Moments**. Transform your goodbye into a toast—a verbal raising of the glass to the evening's shared moments. It's about encapsulating the night's joy, laughter, and camaraderie in a few poignant words, creating a shared memory that those present will cherish and recall with a smile.

> **The Art of Leaving Them Wanting More**. In the city that thrives on intrigue, your parting words should always leave them wanting more. It's about striking a balance between revealing and concealing, giving just enough to pique interest, while holding back enough to maintain an air of mystery.

> **The Personal Touch in Farewells**. Personalize your goodbyes to make them more impactful. A mention of a shared joke, a reference to an earlier conversation, or a complement that's sincere and specific—these touches show that your interactions were meaningful, turning a simple farewell into a personal and memorable connection.

> **Echoes of Your Unique Essence**. Let your parting words be an echo of your unique essence, a verbal signature that's unmistakably you. Whether it's a playful quip, a thoughtful insight, or a flirtatious remark, it should reflect your personality, leaving a lasting impression of who you are.

> **The Promise of Another Encounter**. Lastly, imbue your parting words with the subtle promise of another encounter. Whether it's a casual "See you around" or a more specific "Looking forward to our next adventure," it's about leaving the door open for future rendezvous, sparking anticipation for the next chapter in your Manhattan saga.

In Lasting Impressions in Parting Words, every farewell is an opportunity to leave a part of yourself behind. In a city of millions, your goodbye should be as distinct and unforgettable as your presence, a verbal keepsake that resonates with your unique spirit, ensuring that even in your absence, your essence lingers in the minds of those you've enchanted.

Your Triumphs: Parting Words Activities

_____

_____

_____

_____

_____

_____

_____

_____

_____

_____

_____

_____

_____

_____

_____

_____

_____

_____

_____

_____

Inspirational Quote

IF YOU HAVE GOOD THOUGHTS THEY WILL SHINE OUT OF YOUR FACE LIKE SUNBEAMS, AND YOU WILL ALWAYS LOOK LOVELY. — Roald Dahl

Your Goals: Intentions and Thoughts

The Encore of Elegance

In the pulsating heart of Manhattan, where every moment is a scene waiting to be savored, The Encore of Elegance is about ensuring your exit from any gathering is as captivating as your entrance. It's the art of leaving a lasting impression, a final act that's as graceful and memorable as the opening number.

> ➤ **The Last Act of Glamour**. As the evening winds down, your departure is your encore, your final act of glamour. It's about moving with a grace that turns heads, leaving a trail of admiration in your wake. Whether it's the gentle rustle of your dress or the confident stride in your step, your exit should be a display of effortless elegance, a visual reminder of the poise and charm you've embodied throughout the night.

> ➤ **The Unspoken Promise of Return**. In your farewell lies the unspoken promise of return. It's a subtle art, leaving those you've spent the evening with longing for your next appearance. Your goodbye should be soft yet impactful, a delicate balance that whispers, "This isn't the end, but a pause until we meet again."

> ➤ **The Grace in the Goodbye**. The grace in your goodbye is as important as the warmth in your welcome. It's about maintaining your composure and charm to the very end, ensuring that your final moments in the room are as captivating as your first. A warm smile, a gracious nod, a gentle closing of the door—each a brushstroke in the masterpiece of your evening.

> ➤ **Leaving a Fragrance of Fascination**. As you make your exit, leave behind a fragrance of fascination. It's the subtle scent of your perfume lingering in the air, a sensory souvenir for those you leave behind. It's about ensuring that even in your absence, your presence

is still felt, an aromatic reminder of the elegance and mystery that is quintessentially you.

➤ **The Artful Pause Before Departing**. In the moments before your departure, there's an artful pause, a time when you subtly signal that the evening's chapter is drawing to a close. It's a delicate interlude, filled with appreciative glances and soft exchanges, where your poise sets the tone for a graceful exit.

➤ **The Elegance of Gratitude**. Part of your encore of elegance is the expression of gratitude. A heartfelt "thank you" to the host, a genuine complement on the evening, or a warm acknowledgment of the company you've kept—these gestures of appreciation are the final notes of your presence, resonating with sincerity and style.

➤ **The Choreography of a Graceful Exit**. Just as your entrance was choreographed, so too should your exit be a study in grace. It's the smooth retrieval of your belongings, the unhurried yet purposeful walk to the door, a departure that's as composed as it is captivating, ensuring all eyes are on you until the very end.

➤ **The Lingering Gaze of Farewell**. Lastly, as you step out, leave them with a lingering gaze—a look that speaks volumes, that hints at the depth of the night's experiences and the richness of the connections made. It's a final, silent communication, a gaze that lingers like a soft echo, imprinting your image in the minds of those you leave behind.

In The Encore of Elegance, it's understood that in Manhattan, every exit is an opportunity for an encore, a chance to reaffirm your status as a creature of grace and allure. It's about ensuring that your departure is not a fading note but a resonant chord that leaves the promise of more stories, more laughter, and more enchanting evenings in the city that thrives on encores.

Your Triumphs: Choreographed Exits Activities

_____

_____

_____

_____

_____

_____

_____

_____

_____

_____

_____

_____

_____

_____

_____

_____

_____

_____

_____

_____

_____

_____

_____

_____

Inspirational Quote

MOTIVATION COMES FROM WORKING ON THINGS WE CARE ABOUT. —
Sheryl Sandberg

Your Goals: Intentions and Thoughts

Leaving a Trail of Mystique

In the swirling dance of Manhattan's social ballet, Leaving a Trail of Mystique is about crafting an exit that's as enigmatic as it is elegant. It's the art of departing in a way that leaves a trail of intrigue, a lingering question in the air, a sense of mystery that keeps you etched in the minds of those you leave behind.

➤ **The Enigmatic Smile**. As you prepare to leave, let your smile be your most enigmatic accessory. It's a smile that hints at untold stories, a wordless narrative that leaves others wondering, yearning to know more. It's a smile that promises tales of romance, adventure, and mystery, a silent invitation to be unraveled in future rendezvous.

➤ **The Half-Told Tale**. In your parting words, leave a half-told tale hanging in the air. It's about hinting at a recent adventure or an intriguing plan without giving it all away. Your words should be a tantalizing teaser, a snippet of a story that invites curiosity and speculation.

➤ **The Glimpse of a Secret**. As you gather your things, let there be a glimpse of a secret—a mysterious note tucked in your bag, an unusual trinket, something that piques curiosity. It's these small, seemingly insignificant details that weave an aura of mystery around you, a puzzle that others are compelled to solve.

➤ **The Unanswered Question in Your Goodbye**. Make your goodbye an unanswered question. Whether it's a playful remark left open-ended or a thoughtful comment that hints at deeper layers within, leave them pondering, leave them intrigued, leave them with the irresistible urge to know more.

➤ **The Whispered Farewell**. Infuse your farewells with a tone of secrecy, as if sharing a confidential aside. This whispered goodbye, laden with innuendo, suggests a world of untold stories, leaving those around you intrigued by the mysteries you might hold.

> **The Enigmatic Accessory**. As you depart, let an enigmatic accessory be your silent conversation starter. A vintage brooch, an unusual ring, or an exotic scarf—each piece should be a statement that invites questions and curiosity, a symbol of the mysteries that envelop you.

> **The Unfinished Conversation**. Deliberately leave a conversation unfinished, a thread hanging in the air. It could be an anecdote you start but don't conclude, or a thought you leave tantalizingly open. This deliberate pause creates a space for others to wonder and ponder, drawing them deeper into the enigma that is you.

> **The Veil of Privacy**. In the age of oversharing, maintain a veil of privacy around your personal life. Be selective about what you reveal, sharing just enough to intrigue but never enough to satisfy. This selective sharing makes your presence all the more captivating, a riddle wrapped in the mystery of elegance.

> **The Seductive Glance Back**. As you exit, give a final, fleeting glance back. It's a look that says you're leaving but not gone, a visual promise that there's more to your story. This last glance back should be seductive and suggestive, a silent message that while you're leaving the stage, the play is far from over.

In Leaving a Trail of Mystique, it's not just about the goodbye, but about the promise of more—more stories, more depth, more facets of your intriguing persona yet to be discovered. It's about ensuring that your exit from the evening isn't just a conclusion, but an ellipsis, a to-be-continued in the grand narrative of Manhattan's endless nights. It's an art form, where each departure is a carefully crafted scene, leaving a trail of mystique that winds through the city streets, long after you've disappeared into the night.

Your Triumphs: Manhattan Mystique Activities

Inspirational Quote

EACH PERSON MUST LIVE THEIR LIFE AS A MODEL FOR OTHERS. — Rosa Parks

ENDINGS THAT ECHO

Your Goals: Intentions and Thoughts

Your Goals: Intentions and Thoughts

City Roundup: Manhattan Mystiques – Unraveling Your Inner Self

In the mesmerizing whirlwind that is Manhattan, a city where dreams are woven between skyscrapers and reflected in the Hudson's ripples, "Unlock Manhattan: Master the Art of Lasting Impressions" has been your guide through its enchanting streets. As we draw the curtains with City Roundup: Manhattan Mystiques—Unraveling Your Inner Self, it's time to reflect on the journey we've taken, the secrets we've unlocked, and the myriad ways this city has helped us unravel and discover our inner selves.

Chapters included:

1. A Stride On the Wild Side: Perfecting the Manhattan Walk of Fame

In A Stride On the Wild Side: Perfecting the Manhattan Walk of Fame, it's about transforming every pavement into a stage and every journey into a performance. It's a celebration of movement, a tribute to the individuality and spirit that fuels the city's heartbeat. So, lace up your shoes, darling, and step out into the city—Manhattan awaits your signature stride.

2. Dressed to Distill: Crafting an Ensemble that Whispers Legends

In Dressed to Distill: Crafting an Ensemble that Whispers legends, it's about dressing in a way that transcends the trends of the moment, embracing a style that's steeped in story and significance. It's a celebration of Manhattan's sartorial spirit, where every outfit is a canvas for your personal legend, a way to distill your essence into a look that's as captivating as the city itself. So, step into your wardrobe, darling, and dress not just for the day but for the indelible mark you'll leave on the streets of Manhattan.

3. The Art of Conversation: Mingling with Moxie and Manhattanite Mastery

In The Art of Conversation: Mingling with Moxie and Manhattanite Mastery, it's about wielding words with the same elegance and flair as the city itself. It's a reminder that in Manhattan, a conversation can be as captivating as the skyline—if you know how to navigate its rhythms. So raise your glass, darling, and prepare to enchant with your words, for in the city of endless stories, yours should be told with panache and poise.

4. Eyes that Mesmerize: The Art of the Gaze In the City's Glare

In Eyes that Mesmerize: The Art of the Gaze In the City's Glare, it's about wielding the power of your gaze as effortlessly as you navigate the city streets. It's a reminder that in the land of skyscrapers and star lights, your eyes can be your most powerful tool—a way to connect, to captivate, and to communicate without saying a single word. So, darling, as you step out into the night, remember that your gaze can be as enchanting as the Manhattan skyline itself.

5. The Sound of Silence: Knowing When to Pause and Power Up the Intrigue

In The Sound of Silence: Knowing When to Pause and Power Up the Intrigue, it's about embracing the quiet amidst the chaos, finding strength in stillness. It's a reminder that in the endless soundtrack of Manhattan, the most memorable notes are sometimes those that are never played. So, as you navigate the city's endless symphony, remember that your silence can be as commanding as your speech, a space where the unsung melodies of intrigue and allure reside.

6. Glamour On the Go:
New York Nights and Taxi Cab Confessions

In Glamour On the Go: New York Nights and Taxi Cab Confessions, the journey through Manhattan's streets becomes as enchanting as the destination. It's about embracing the unexpected, the conversations and connections that can arise in the transient space of a taxi cab, turning a simple ride into an unforgettable part of your New York story. So, darling, as you slide into the backseat and the city unfolds before you, remember: every ride is an opportunity for a new tale, a new confession, a new chapter in the ongoing saga of Manhattan.

7. Rooftop Reveries:
Rising Above and Holding Court with the Stars

In this chapter, Rooftop Reveries: Rising Above and Holding Court with the Stars, the experience of Manhattan's rooftop culture is elevated into a poetic narrative, capturing the allure, the romance, and the magic of being perched atop the city that never sleeps. It's a testament to the power of place in shaping our experiences and the enchanting possibilities that await when we dare to ascend.

8. Boutique Brilliance: Discovering the City's Best-Kept Secrets
In Boutique Brilliance: Discovering the City's Best-Kept Secrets, the journey is more than a shopping spree; it's an exploration of Manhattan's heart and soul, told through its fashion boutiques. Each visit, each find, each piece of clothing is a chapter in the larger story of the city—a story of creativity, individuality, and the timeless allure of discovering something truly unique.

9. Dinner Dates and Late-Night Fates: Manhattan's Recipe for Unforgettable Evenings

In Dinner Dates and Late-Night Fates: Manhattan's Recipe for Unforgettable Evenings, the essence of the city's dining scene is more than just about food; it's a stage for romance, a canvas for fashion, and a gateway to adventures. It's an exploration of how, in the right setting, with the right person, a simple dinner date can transform into an unforgettable chapter in the story of your life.

10. Endings that Echo: Ensuring Your Exit Is as Memorable as Your Entrance

In Endings that Echo: Ensuring Your Exist Is as Memorable as Your Entrance, the philosophy is simple yet profound: in Manhattan, every exit is an art, a final note in the evening's melody that should resonate with grace, elegance, and an enticing promise of future tales. It's a reminder that in the city of endless stories, your farewell is just the prelude to your next grand entrance.

But, my dear, the greatest discovery in Unlock Manhattan" has been about ourselves. In learning to navigate the city's mystique, we've also learned to navigate our own complexities. Manhattan, with its unending energy and its kaleidoscopic moments, mirrors our own desires, fears, ambitions, and dreams. It teaches us to embrace our multifaceted selves, to find our rhythm in its chaos, and to make every step, every glance, every word, a part of our own grand narrative.

As we conclude this journey with City Roundup, remember that Manhattan is more than a backdrop; it's a catalyst for self-discovery. It's a city that challenges you to be bold, to be vulnerable, to be unapologetically you. So, darling, as you walk its streets, let it unlock your potential, your passions, your stories. Because in the end, mastering the art of lasting impressions in Manhattan is about mastering the art of being wonderfully, irrevocably, uniquely you.

Where Do We Go from Here?

As we close the vibrant pages of "Unlock Manhattan: Master the Art of Lasting Impressions," the first enthralling step in our journey through The Manhattan Diaries, we find ourselves at a tantalizing crossroads. With the city's secrets beginning to unfold before us, the question that dances in the air, as electric as Times Square at midnight, is Where Do We Go from Here?

In the next chapter of our Manhattan saga, "Behind the Velvet Rope: NYC's Grooming Secrets Revealed," we prepare to delve deeper into the heart of the city's allure. We've mastered the art of making lasting impressions, of weaving our presence into the very fabric of Manhattan's streets. Now, darling, it's time to unravel the mysteries behind the city's impeccable style and grace, the grooming secrets that keep its inhabitants as dazzling as the skyline itself.

"Behind the Velvet Rope" is an odyssey into the sanctuaries of sophistication hidden in plain sight, from the plush salons of the Upper East Side to the bespoke barbershops in Brooklyn. It's a journey into the rituals and routines that define Manhattan's chic, an exploration of the self care regimes that empower its people to walk with confidence, charm, and charisma.

But as we embark on this next phase, remember, our journey through The Manhattan Diaries is more than a mere makeover. It's about the transformation within, the redefining of self that occurs when you not only look but feel your best. "Behind the Velvet Rope" is about discovering the grooming rituals that resonate with your personal style, about finding your unique rhythm in the city's symphony of sophistication.

So, where do we go from here? We step behind the velvet rope, into a world of refinement and elegance, a world where grooming is an art and self care a statement. We continue our journey through The Manhattan Diaries, not just to reinvent our exteriors but to uncover a side of ourselves that even Manhattan has yet to see.

In this 21-step odyssey, each book, each chapter, each page is a step closer to the most authentic, polished version of ourselves. So, let's turn the page, darling, with anticipation and excitement for the secrets yet to be revealed, for the transformation yet to be experienced in the captivating journey that is The Manhattan Diaries.

Your Triumphs: Recap Activities

Inspirational Quote

ACT AS IF WHAT YOU DO MAKES A DIFFERENCE. IT DOES. — William James

Your Goals: Intentions and Thoughts

Journal Pages: Pen Your Tales

Journal Pages: Pen Your Tales

Journal Pages: Pen Your Tales

Journal Pages: Pen Your Tales

Journal Pages: Pen Your Tales

Journal Pages: Pen Your Tales

Journal Pages: Pen Your Tales

Journal Pages: Pen Your Tales

Journal Pages: Pen Your Tales

Journal Pages: Pen Your Tales

www.ingramcontent.com/pod-product-compliance
Lightning Source LLC
Chambersburg PA
CBHW032054020426
42335CB00011B/329